FIVE PLAYS

FOR GIRLS AND BOYS TO PERFORM

TEACHER'S GUIDE AND SCRIPTS

Tea for Felicity
Home Is Where the Heart Is
Friendship and Freedom
Actions Speak Louder Than Words
War on the Home Front

Published by Pleasant Company Publications

For information, address: Book Editor, Pleasant Company Publications, 8400 Fairway Place, P.O. Box 620998, Middleton, WI 53562.

First Edition.
Printed in the United States of America.
97 98 99 WCR 10 9 8 7 6 5 4 3 2

PICTURE CREDITS
The following organizations have generously given permission to reprint illustrations:
Page 90—Bayside Plantation Records, Southern Historical Collection, University of North Carolina, Chapel Hill (banjos); 97—George Eastman House; 99—Museum of the City of New York, Theatre Collection; 127—Harvard Theatre Collection.

Special thanks to
Pauline Devins Marth, Director, St. Thomas Day School, Columbus, GA; and Cathy McKinley, Fourth-Grade Teacher, and Carol Diers Spiegel, Third-Grade Teacher, Randall Elementary School, Madison, WI.

Plays adapted by Valerie Tripp from the following books in The American Girls Collection:
Tea for Felicity adapted from *Felicity Learns a Lesson,* by Valerie Tripp.
Home Is Where the Heart Is adapted from *Meet Kirsten,* by Janet Shaw.
Friendship and Freedom adapted from *Addy Learns a Lesson,* by Connie Porter.
Actions Speak Louder Than Words adapted from *Meet Samantha,* by Susan S. Adler.
War on the Home Front adapted from *Meet Molly,* by Valerie Tripp.

Teacher's guide written by Tamara England, Jeanne E. Harrison, and Lynda Sharpe
Edited by Tamara England
Designed by Kym Abrams and Julie Mierkiewicz
Produced by Karen Bennett, Laura Paulini, Sue Thorsen, and Pat Tuchscherer

Library of Congress Cataloging-in-Publication Data

Tripp, Valerie, 1951–
Five plays for girls and boys to perform : teacher's guide and scripts / [Valerie Tripp]. — 1st ed.
p. cm. — (The American girls collection)
Contents: Tea for felicity — Home is where the heart is — Friendship and freedom — Actions speak louder than words — War on the home front.

ISBN 1-56247-234-8
1. Girls—United States—Juvenile drama. 2. Historical drama, American.
3. Children's plays, American. [1. United States—History—Drama. 2. Plays.] I. Title. II. Series.
PS3570.R545F58 1995 812'.54—dc20 95-35214 CIP AC

Contents

Overview

Tea for Felicity
Colonial America – 1774

Home Is Where the Heart Is
Immigration to America – 1854

Friendship and Freedom
Civil War America – 1864

Actions Speak Louder Than Words
America's New Century – 1904

War on the Home Front
World War Two America – 1944

Appendixes

OVERVIEW

Introduction

Five Plays contains reproducible play scripts of five plays featuring the characters in The American Girls Collection®, a series of historical fiction set in five important time periods in America's past. The plays are written at a third-grade level—but are adaptable for both older and younger students—and appeal to both girls and boys. Each play is approximately twenty minutes long and can be performed easily in a classroom.

The plays feature Felicity, Kirsten, Addy, Samantha, and Molly, who are bright, lively nine-year-old girls. Some of your students may have read some of the historical fiction on which these plays are based and will enjoy the plays because they enjoy the books and the characters. But students who have not read the stories will also enjoy the plays, which can stand alone and are important for both the drama they offer and the history they teach.

Using Drama in Your Classroom

Integrating your social studies curriculum with literature and drama can bring history to life. Literature offers a window to another world—it allows children to try life on for size within the security of the classroom or their home. Drama takes that important experience a step further—it allows children to become the characters that bring a story or history to life. By dramatically re-creating an episode from a story or from history, children can learn history in an exciting way.

Drama has long been included in language arts programs because it naturally integrates the language arts skills of

The Plays

Tea for Felicity *is set in 1774 in Williamsburg, Virginia, when American colonists were struggling with the conflicting needs of independence and loyalty to England.*

Home Is Where the Heart Is *is the story of a dramatic journey in 1854 filled with hardships and hope—a story shared by many of the immigrants who have come to settle in America.*

Friendship and Freedom *is set in Philadelphia in 1864—near the end of the Civil War—when many families were separated by slavery and the country was bitterly divided by the war.*

Actions Speak Louder Than Words *takes place in 1904 and highlights America's new century—and the many changes brought about by rapid industrialization.*

War on the Home Front *shows how Americans on the home front in World War Two coped with wartime shortages and worried about loved ones fighting far away.*

Themes in the Plays

- *Change*
- *Friendship*
- *Families*
- *Loyalty*
- *Independence*
- *Communication*
- *Conflict and conflict resolution*

Reader's Theater

In reader's theater, the drama is created almost entirely by voice. Actors read the parts with expression and portray the characters through voice and occasional sound effects. There are few or no actions.

listening and speaking, reading and writing, and analysis. A performance involves listening and speaking. Learning a role requires reading and memorizing a script. Creating a believable performance involves analysis and understanding of characters and relationships. Finally, reflection on and discussion of a character, situation, or whole performance involves more analysis—and may include writing and additional dramatization. Throughout all of these activities, comprehension is repeatedly tested and deepened.

By bringing drama into history or social studies, you can help your students learn about history in a way that is personal and real—and lasting. As they perform the roles of characters from the past, they will feel what it was like to live long ago and will understand in a personal way why certain things happened as they did.

Using These Plays in Your Classroom

For a language arts project, you may want to divide your class into five groups and assign one play to each group. For a social studies unit, you may decide to use only one or two plays related to time periods you are studying.

Each play has parts for six actors, but may be staged with only four or five actors if some actors play more than one part. Students can stage the plays independently in small groups and perform for the rest of the class, or the whole class can produce one or several plays together, with all students involved as actors or crew members. If your school has an auditorium and stage, a performance of one or more of the plays for the rest of the school may be an exciting project for your students. The plays may also be performed as reader's theater, which involves creating the drama by voice alone, with little or no action.

For an extracurricular activity, one drama teacher produced plays from this book by having high school drama club students direct grade school students in several of the plays for an all-school spring program. Other teachers have produced the plays successfully with students in after-school programs.

The reproducible scripts and other blackline masters provide the information and direction your students need to independently plan for and stage the plays. Following each script is a set of blackline masters about the characters, costumes, sets, and props for that play, along with some general information about the director, the crew, and the stage.

Finally, there is a related activity for each play that allows your students to say in their own words what they believe or understand about some of the issues raised in the plays. The activities involve the whole class and give all students the chance to act in a voice and persona from the past. Because they allow everyone to experience first-hand conflicts and issues that are either explicit or implicit in the plays, these activities often stimulate rich and lively discussions, especially as part of a social studies unit.

Involving All Students

Drama gives all students a chance to participate. Students who are usually withdrawn may suddenly shine in character. And for students who love being the center of attention, drama can channel that energy and focus it into meaningful interaction.

Involving the Boys in the Class

Boys enjoy these plays as much as girls do. By expecting the boys in your class to read and participate in the plays, you make that enjoyment acceptable. Remind your students that drama and acting are about belief—actors do not need to look like the characters they are playing, but they do need to believe in and act like the characters.

Each of the plays—except *Friendship and Freedom*—has at least one male part. If boys are not comfortable acting in female roles, they can participate in the play as crew members and through the related activities. You may also add male roles by writing in male parts, or by having the boys in your class be extras. Remind your students that in some periods of history—and in some theatrical traditions even today—males have played all parts, female as well as male.

Involving Students from Diverse Backgrounds

Encourage all students to try for the role they want, regardless of gender, ethnicity, or race. Any child may play any role.

Ways to Involve Boys

- *Expect them to read the plays.*
- *Put each play in its historical context.*
- *Discuss the male characters in the plays.*
- *Encourage them to try out for any role they'd like.*
- *Encourage them to write other male roles into the plays.*
- *Encourage active participation as crew members.*
- *Suggest that boys write and act in a play about a boy living at the time of the play.*

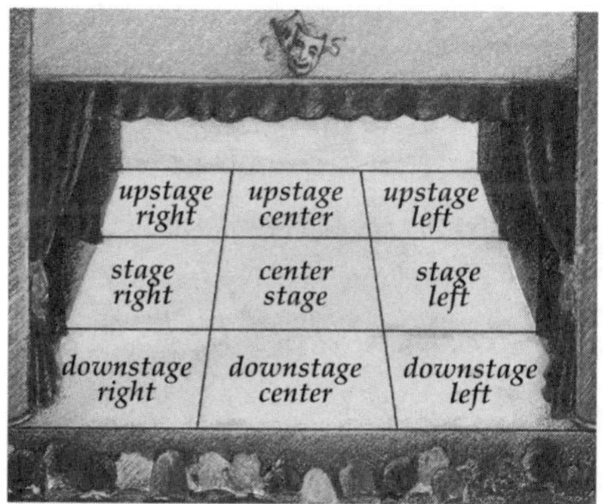

Stage Vocabulary

Stages used to be built on a slant, with the back higher than the front. This allowed the audience to see the actors better. The terms ***upstage*** *and* ***downstage*** *come from the way the stage slanted.* ***Upstage*** *is the back of the stage, which used to be higher.* ***Downstage*** *is the front of the stage, nearest the audience. An actor standing in the exact middle of the stage is at* ***center stage.***

The best way to help your students remember ***stage right*** *and* ***stage left*** *is to have them face the audience.*

Each "Putting on the Play" section includes information about the stage (see pages 32, 63, 93, 124, and 153).

The Related Activities

The additional activities in this book help students develop a greater understanding of the time periods in which the plays take place and some of the central issues in the plays. Students can brainstorm in groups and act out scenes, either before or after performing the plays. The activities will help students think more critically, build trust and rapport as a group, and allow them to explore their own feelings about conflicts and issues related to those in the plays.

The Teacher's Role in the Related Activities

If you decide to use some or all of the related activities, you can structure your role in two ways. As a facilitator, your role would be fairly traditional—to mediate discussions and assign tasks. As a participant, you would stimulate discussion and introduce challenging conflicts within the context of the activity.

As a facilitator, you can ask questions, mediate discussion, and keep students on task. You could also focus student work by *sidecoaching*. The purpose of sidecoaching is to improve the work without stopping it. You can call out questions and remarks to sharpen the students' work, such as, "Remember, Samantha doesn't know you're there," "*Silently* show us what is happening." Students should hear the instruction and continue with their scene, amending it as necessary.

You may also direct the activity by actually participating in some of the dramatic improvisation. Teachers who are comfortable improvising with their students will find that students generally increase their commitment to the activity when they see their teacher modeling commitment. Students tend to enjoy improvisations more if they get to watch and interact with their teacher in a role. They feel able to take more risks if they feel that everyone—including the teacher—is taking a risk and pretending together.

Drama Vocabulary

You can introduce these terms to students as they prepare to read or perform the plays.

ad-lib: *to improvise or make up lines spontaneously*

blackout: *a turning off of stage lighting while actors are onstage*

blocking: *to plan onstage movement*

cue: *a signal to an actor or crew member*

fade-out/in: *a gradual decrease or increase of the volume or lighting*

frozen image: *a moment chosen to show a dramatic incident or suggest an important message*

improvisation: *spontaneously making up or inventing lines or action*

intermission: *a short break between acts of a play*

pantomime: *to tell a story or convey a message with movement alone*

props/properties: *items actors hold or use onstage*

tableau: *see "frozen image"*

As a participant, you can control students from within the context of the activity. For example, when doing the activity related to Molly's play, instead of interrupting an unfocused scene to impose discipline as the teacher, you may impose order as the radio show producer. By doing so, you reinforce the seriousness of the improvisation through your commitment to your role and the given circumstances of the activity.

If you don't have a lot of experience in creative dramatics, talk to other teachers who have used drama or creative dramatics in the classroom to see what has worked well for them. And if you are not comfortable participating in a role, you can easily lead all the activities as the facilitator. However you decide to incorporate the plays and the activities into your curriculum, all may be easily modified and expanded to meet your needs and those of your students.

Students from Middleton, Wisconsin, in a performance of ***War on the Home Front.***

ABOUT THE PLAYWRIGHT

Valerie Tripp wrote all of the plays in The American Girls Collection. She is also the author of the Felicity and Molly books and three of the Samantha books. Ms. Tripp enjoys writing plays because she believes that children learn best by doing, participating, and acting.

Students interested in learning more about the playwright will enjoy a videotape of Ms. Tripp being interviewed by 5th-grade students, which is available from Pleasant Company. To order, call 1-800-350-6555.

TEA FOR FELICITY

COLONIAL AMERICA—1774

FELICITY ❧ 1774

In 1774, many American colonists were struggling for independence from England. Felicity was struggling for independence, too—while trying to remain loyal to her family and friends.

ABOUT THE PLAY

Tea for Felicity is a play about Felicity Merriman, a fictional nine-year-old girl growing up in Williamsburg, Virginia, just as the American Revolution is starting.

In colonial times, girls did not usually go to school. They were taught to read and write at home—if they learned to read and write at all. But it was important for girls to master the skills of a gentlewoman—the management of a household, fine stitchery, penmanship, and the proper way to serve tea.

In *Tea for Felicity*, Felicity has just started taking lessons from Miss Manderly. There she meets Elizabeth and her sister Annabelle, who have recently arrived from England, and who are also taking lessons from Miss Manderly. Felicity and Elizabeth quickly become good friends, but Felicity and Annabelle clash. At her lessons, Felicity comes to love serving tea and the tea ceremony, an English custom still much practiced and valued by the colonists. In fact, many of the customs and things the colonists valued came from England.

Felicity and her family have always been ruled by King George of England. But in 1774, changes are in the air. Many colonists, called Patriots, want independence from the king. Other colonists—Loyalists—support the king's rule over the colonies. Felicity is from a Patriot family. To protest a tax the king has placed on tea, Felicity's father refuses to buy or sell tea in his store, or to drink tea at home. But Felicity's new friend Elizabeth is from a Loyalist family.

Felicity is torn between loyalty to her Patriot father and loyalty to Elizabeth. She loves the tea ceremony but does not want to betray her father and the Patriots' cause by drinking tea. She also longs to speak her mind and to get even with snobby Annabelle, but she wants to do so politely and with civility, as she is being taught by Miss Manderly. Elizabeth, too, feels the strain of divided loyalties, between her love for her own family and her affection and respect for her Patriot friend.

The personal conflicts that Felicity and Elizabeth feel mirror the conflicts the colonists faced. Personal affections and loyalties were often divided because of the intense political issues of the day. In *Tea for Felicity,* Felicity must learn to find her own way through the conflicts. Reading and dramatizing this play will help your students understand how historic events affect individuals—even children—firsthand and personally. The related activity will help your students experience for themselves some of the issues at the heart of the conflict and will help them approach the play more meaningfully, both as performers and as audience members.

Historical Context

In 1763, England defeated France in the French and Indian War, and as a result, England controlled much of North America. But the war had been costly. England needed money to cover its debts and wanted the colonies to help pay the debt through taxes. Despite protests by the colonists against taxation without representation, the English Parliament levied numerous taxes on the colonies. When England passed the Stamp Act in 1765, which taxed printed documents, and the Townshend Acts in 1767, which levied taxes on tea and other imported goods, the colonists were furious. Protests against England's policies periodically erupted into violence. Events like the 1770 Boston Massacre and the 1773 Boston Tea Party further deepened the anger of the colonists and strengthened their determination to free themselves from the rule of England. Citizens and merchants like Felicity's father signed petitions agreeing to boycott tea and other English goods. But as the number and frequency of the protests increased, the division among neighbors, friends, and even family members increased, too.

Finally, in 1774, the colonies met as a united front in the First Continental Congress. They sent their protests to King George, who refused their requests. The king declared the colonies "in rebellion" and the colonies declared themselves independent in the Declaration of Independence. In 1775, the Battles of Lexington and Concord marked the beginning of the Revolutionary War.

The Terms Colonist, Patriot, and Loyalist

Colonists *were all the residents of the thirteen English colonies.* ***Patriots*** *were colonists who wanted freedom from rule by the king of England.* ***Loyalists*** *wanted the colonists to remain under the king's rule.*

The Ambivalence of the Colonists

At the time the Declaration of Independence was signed in 1776, there were 2.5 million colonists in America. About one third considered themselves neutral, reflecting their ambivalence about English rule. Another third considered themselves Patriots, and one third considered themselves Loyalists.

Historical Events Made Personal

Political issues of the day come to life in Felicity's activities and decisions. At her lessons at Miss Manderly's home, Felicity finds herself faced with the issue of how to be loyal to both her father and her friend. She must also decide how to be polite—as she has been taught—and still stand up for herself and her beliefs.

THEMES IN THE PLAY

Tea for Felicity would obviously fit in well in a social studies or history unit on colonial life or on the Revolutionary War. But the play could also be included in thematic units on friendship, family, change, loyalty, the need for independence, the education of girls and boys, and conflict and conflict resolution.

PREPARING TO PERFORM—A TOWN MEETING

This activity can be done either before or after reading or performing the play to help your students get more from the play. It will help students learn more about the differences between Loyalists and Patriots, and deepen students' understanding of Felicity's predicament in the play *Tea for Felicity.*

A TOWN MEETING

Objectives:
To understand and express Loyalist and Patriot opinions

To speak in a voice different from one's own, recognizing that different tones of speech are appropriate for different occasions and time periods

To negotiate with others whose viewpoints differ

To interact in a role and with others in role

Teacher's Role: *Participant, in role as a community leader*

Student Roles: *The citizens of Williamsburg, Virginia, in 1774*

Time Needed: *30 minutes*

Space Needed: *An open area large enough for a "town meeting"*

Materials Needed: *Cards or slips of paper with roles on them; blank paper and a quill or pen*

Context

It is 1774, shortly after the Boston Tea Party, and the citizens of Williamsburg are assembled to discuss whether the community as a whole should support the rule of the king of England or support the tea boycott.

Directions

1. Prepare materials: Write roles on index cards. Use familiar roles from the play, such as the Angry Man, Mr. Merriman, and Miss Manderly, and create roles of other Williamsburg residents, such as the milliner, the barber, a gentleman, etc. Be sure to note whether they are Patriots, Loyalists, or undecided (e.g., "Loyalist blacksmith" or "Patriot apothecary").

Roll up and tie a blank piece of paper. Find a calligraphy pen or—for authenticity—a quill pen and ink with which to draft a letter.

2. Hand out roles: Introduce this as an activity in which your students will go into roles to discuss why they think the colonies should or should not support the boycott. Have your students draw cards or choose roles to play. Explain that they must develop the rationale behind their characters' political beliefs. They should use their own prior knowledge and their imaginations to create the logic behind their characters' views.

3. The town meeting: Your role is as a community leader. You have been asked by Parliament to write a letter denouncing the boycott and confirming

Williamsburg's support of British rule. You have invited the assembled townspeople to voice their opinions and advise you what to say in the letter. In your role, you will be primarily concerned with eliciting opinions and encouraging negotiation between the opposing parties. Your character would ask clarifying and probing questions to gather accurate details for the letter that is to be written after the meeting.

Assemble the "townspeople" for the meeting and assume your role. Begin the discussion by reminding them of the letter you've been asked to write. You could start with a voice vote to determine whether to support King George or support the tea boycott. After the vote, ask each citizen to explain his or her vote. Encourage discussion and arguments from both sides until all the townspeople have been heard. Then ask the assembly what you should do about the petition: "A response is required. What should the letter say?"

4. Resolution: The townspeople should provide suggestions, including any of the following: consensus must be reached; a compromise must be found; the majority rules and those holding the minority view will be fined; or no resolution can be agreed upon. You can actually draft the letter at the meeting, designate a committee to draft the letter, or tell the assembly that you will return when you have finished the letter. Then adjourn the meeting.

5. Discussion and reflection: Ask everyone to come out of role to discuss the meeting. Was it difficult for the students to rationalize—in role—a position they did not agree with? Did anyone change his or her mind during the debate? Can they understand how this disagreement and others like it eventually led the country into war? Why or why not?

You could also explain that in 1774 women might not have attended such a meeting. What do they think women might have been thinking about at home while their husbands, fathers, and sons decided the future of the country?

An Alternative

An alternative way to do this activity would be to hand out all roles randomly and then to ask those with female roles to stand around the edges of the meeting space and watch silently while those with male roles express their opinions and vote.

Compare the fact that women don't have a vote with the idea that the colonists don't have a voice through representation. Conclude with a discussion about how it felt to be included or excluded from the decision-making process.

Tea for Felicity

A Play About Felicity

Play Script

TIPS FOR ACTORS

❧ Use your imagination. If you don't have a fancy stage or elaborate props and costumes, act as if you do!

❧ Speak clearly and loudly enough to be heard. Don't turn your back to the audience or stand between another actor and the audience.

❧ Pretend that you **are** the character you are playing. If you forget your lines and can't hear the prompter, think about what the character would really say and say it in your own words.

❧ Act and speak at the same time. Directions before your lines will tell you things to do as you are saying those lines. For example,

> *(**Felicity** bites the biscuit, then jumps up, hand to cheek, wailing.)*
>
> **FELICITY:** Oooh! Ow!

❧ Other directions make suggestions about how to say a line. For example,

> **ANNABELLE:** *(angrily)* Fun? You have no manners!

❧ Cooperate with the director and the other actors. And don't forget to smile at the curtain call!

TEA FOR FELICITY

A Play About Felicity

CHARACTERS

FELICITY
A nine-year-old girl growing up just before the American Revolution

FATHER
Felicity's father, a merchant who disagrees with the king

MISS MANDERLY
Felicity's teacher

ELIZABETH
A shy nine-year-old girl from England, who is Felicity's best friend

ANNABELLE
Elizabeth's snobby older sister

ANGRY MAN
A man who is angry at Felicity's father for disagreeing with the king

The action takes place in the fall of 1774, in Williamsburg, the capital of the king's colony of Virginia.

ACT ONE

Scene: Miss Manderly's parlor. Miss Manderly, Annabelle, and Elizabeth sit at the tea table.

(***Felicity*** *ENTERS.)*

MISS MANDERLY: *(nodding and smiling at Felicity)* Good day, Miss Merriman. How lovely to meet you. I am Miss Manderly.

FELICITY: *(curtsies)* Good day, Miss Manderly. Thank you very much indeed for having me.

MISS MANDERLY: You are most welcome. Now I will introduce you to the other young ladies. They have just arrived in Virginia from England. This is Miss Annabelle Cole. And this is Miss Elizabeth Cole.

ANNABELLE: Oh, don't bother to call her Elizabeth. She's such a little bit of a thing, we call her *Bitsy* at home.

(***Elizabeth*** *looks unhappy.)*

FELICITY: Good day, Annabelle. Good day...Elizabeth.

(***Elizabeth*** *smiles as* ***Felicity*** *sits at the tea table.)*

ANNABELLE: *(snobbishly)* Your name is Merriman. You must be the shopkeeper's daughter. In England, Bitsy and I had our *own* governess. I never thought we'd have to share lessons with a shopkeeper's daughter.

FELICITY: *(proudly)* My father's store is the finest in Williamsburg!

MISS MANDERLY: *(firmly)* Young ladies. *(She pauses as all three girls bow their heads in embarrassment.)* Your parents have asked me to teach you the rules of polite behavior. Manners are observed most closely at tea. I will now instruct you in the proper way to serve tea.

ANNABELLE: *(rolling her eyes)* Good heavens! Bitsy and I know how to serve tea! We've watched Mama serve tea hundreds of times!

MISS MANDERLY: Splendid! Then you will be quite at ease, won't you?

*(**Annabelle** huffs.)*

MISS MANDERLY: Watch closely, ladies. I will ask each of you to serve the tea soon.

*(They watch as **Miss Manderly** gracefully opens the tea caddy, spoons tea leaves into the pot, pours water from the kettle onto the leaves, and gently swishes the pot to mix the water and tea together. She hands each girl a cup, saucer, and spoon and pours the tea as she says…)*

MISS MANDERLY: When the tea is ready, pour it very carefully. Offer your guest milk and sugar to put in her tea. Then offer her something to eat. *(picking up a plate)* Annabelle, would you care for a cake?

ANNABELLE: Oh, these are queen cakes! The queen of England likes these. *(She greedily takes quite a few from the plate.)*

MISS MANDERLY: *(looking directly at Annabelle)* Remember, young ladies, you aren't eating because you're hungry or drinking because you're thirsty. *(to Felicity and Elizabeth)* The tea is offered to you as a sign of your hostess's hospitality. If you refuse tea, you are refusing her generosity.

FELICITY: *(sincerely)* Oh, I'd never refuse! You make the tea ceremony look so pretty.

MISS MANDERLY: Thank you, my dear. But you may not wish to drink tea all afternoon! There is, of course, a polite way to show that you do not wish to take more tea. Merely turn your cup upside down on your saucer and place your spoon across it. *(demonstrating)* And the correct phrase to say is, "Thank you. I shall take no tea."

FELICITY: Oh, dear...there is so much to remember!

MISS MANDERLY: Indeed, yes. A gentlewoman must know what to do in any situation. And now, young ladies, excuse me for a moment. All the queen cakes are gone. *(She picks up the empty plate and stands up.)*

*(**Miss Manderly** EXITS.)*

ANNABELLE: *(in a mean voice, as soon as Miss Manderly has left)* Well, of course, soon we won't have *any* tea to drink if these uncivilized colonists have their way.

FELICITY: *(puzzled)* What do you mean?

ANNABELLE: Haven't you heard? A few days ago in Yorktown, a mob of colonists threw chests of tea from an English ship into the river.

FELICITY: But why did they do that?

ANNABELLE: Because they are hotheads! Simply a wild mob!

ELIZABETH: *(softly, to Felicity)* They didn't hurt anybody.

ANNABELLE: *(glaring at Elizabeth)* Quiet, Bitsy! *(to Felicity)* The colonists destroyed the tea because they didn't want to pay the king's tax on it. You colonists are *so* uncivilized. You are ungrateful for all our king has done. You...

*(**Annabelle** stops suddenly when **Miss Manderly** ENTERS with a plate of biscuits.)*

MISS MANDERLY: Felicity, would you like a biscuit?

FELICITY: Yes, thank you, ma'am.

(***Felicity*** *bites the biscuit, then jumps up, hand to cheek, wailing.)*

FELICITY: Oooh! Ow!

(***Annabelle*** *shrieks and jumps up onto her chair, as if afraid of a mouse.* ***Elizabeth*** *says "Oops!" as some of the silverware or silver pieces from the tea tray crash to the floor.)*

MISS MANDERLY: *(exclaims)* Ladies, ladies! Calm yourselves! Now! Miss Merriman, please tell us what happened.

FELICITY: I…well, it's my tooth…my loose tooth. It fell out when I bit into the biscuit and it…it fell into my tea! I'm so sorry, I…

ANNABELLE: *(wrinkling her nose in disgust)* Oh! How uncivilized! How rude!

MISS MANDERLY: *(kindly)* Don't fret, my dear. There was no harm done. I suppose a gentlewoman should know what to say in any situation. But I must admit, I don't know what to say when a tooth falls into the tea!

(***Annabelle*** *scowls, but* ***Miss Manderly, Elizabeth,*** *and* ***Felicity*** *laugh happily.)*

ACT TWO

Scene: The Merrimans' store, two weeks later. Elizabeth is standing and looking on as Felicity sits in a chair carefully stitching her sampler.

ELIZABETH: Your sampler looks pretty, Felicity! We've been having lessons for only two weeks, and your stitchery has improved a lot!

FELICITY: I still don't like stitchery very much. But I do love our lessons at Miss Manderly's. *(smiles at Elizabeth)* Mostly I love them because of *you*. I'm glad you're my friend, Elizabeth.

ELIZABETH: I'm glad, too. *(plopping down in another chair)* Shall I tell you a secret? Annabelle is sweet on Ben. She thinks he's handsome!

FELICITY: Ben? My father's apprentice? Oh, that's too funny!

*(They giggle. **Father** ENTERS.)*

FATHER: Well, here are the two merriest girls in Virginia. *(He crosses to them.)* And what are you laughing about today?

FELICITY: Oh, we're just sharing a secret, Father.

*(Suddenly there is loud knocking at the door. The **Angry Man** ENTERS, waving a piece of paper that is a petition with many signatures.)*

ANGRY MAN: *(loudly)* Mr. Merriman! What is the meaning of this, sir?

*(**Elizabeth** and **Felicity** get up and back out of the way. They look worried.)*

FATHER: *(calmly)* Yes, I signed that agreement. More than four hundred other merchants signed it, too. We have decided not to sell tea anymore. It is our way of showing the king we disagree with his tax on tea.

ANGRY MAN: That is disloyal! It is wrong for colonists to go against the king! You know it is wrong, Merriman.

FATHER: *(firmly)* Sir! I have to do what I think is *right*.

ANGRY MAN: And what of those hotheads in Yorktown? Do you think they were right when they tossed good tea into the river?

FATHER: They threw that tea away to send a message to the king. They did what they thought was right.

*(**Elizabeth,** clearly upset by these words, EXITS by slipping quietly out the door.)*

*(**Felicity** is listening to the conversation and does not notice Elizabeth's departure.)*

ANGRY MAN: They were wrong to toss that tea! And you are wrong to stop selling tea. You are making a grave mistake. *(crossing to the door)* No Loyalist will ever shop in your store again! We won't give our business to a merchant who isn't loyal to the king.

FATHER: *(kindly)* Sir, you are my neighbor and my friend. Can't we disagree politely, without fighting? Fighting does no good.

ANGRY MAN: Humph! Good day to you, sir!

*(**Angry Man** EXITS, storming out.)*

FELICITY: *(sees Elizabeth is gone, runs to Father)* Father! That man frightened Elizabeth so much she ran away! Who was he?

FATHER: He is a Loyalist. He is angry because I've decided to stop selling tea in my store, to show the king we colonists will not pay his tax.

FELICITY: If no one pays the tax, it will make the king angry. Won't that start a fight?

FATHER: *(nodding his head sadly)* Aye. It could.

FELICITY: Do you think there will be a war?

FATHER: I hope not.

FELICITY: *(slowly)* Father, will we drink tea at home?

FATHER: No. There will be no tea in our house.

FELICITY: But what should I do at lessons? We drink tea there. *(pauses)* And teatime is so very important. What will Miss Manderly think if I refuse tea?

*(**Felicity** looks sad. **Father** hugs her.)*

ACT THREE

Scene: Miss Manderly's parlor, the next day. Felicity and Miss Manderly are standing by the table.

*(**Annabelle** and **Elizabeth** ENTER.)*

MISS MANDERLY: Ah, Annabelle and Elizabeth, good morning!

ANNABELLE and **ELIZABETH:** *(curtsying)* Good morning, Miss Manderly.

MISS MANDERLY: Elizabeth and Felicity, you may be seated. I'd like you to work on your samplers. *(They sit at the tea table.)* Annabelle, come with me, please. We'll work on your handwriting.

ANNABELLE: *(snobbishly, as she hangs up her hat)* Good! It's so tiresome when I'm with Bitsy and that Merriman girl. My handwriting is so much better than theirs.

*(**Miss Manderly** and **Annabelle** EXIT.)*

*(**Felicity** grins at Elizabeth and rolls her eyes about Annabelle. But **Elizabeth** looks down at her sampler and will not smile. With a mischievous look, **Felicity** gets up and puts on Annabelle's hat. She minces over to Elizabeth, batting her eyelashes and imitating Annabelle's voice, saying…)*

FELICITY: Oh! Ben! It is I, your beautiful Bananabelle!

ELIZABETH: *(giggles)* Bananabelle? Oh, Annabelle…Bananabelle! *(looks toward the door nervously)* Do be careful, Lissie! If Annabelle saw you, she'd be angry. And she can be mean. I'm afraid of her.

FELICITY: *(in her own voice)* Oh, I am not afraid of Annabelle Bananabelle!

*(**Annabelle** ENTERS and stands in the doorway scowling. Neither girl sees her.)*

FELICITY: *(imitating Annabelle's voice and clasping her hands near her heart dramatically)* Oh, my darling Ben! Say that you love your Bananabelle! You know you have stolen my heart away! Let us be married! Oh, I love you, you handsome lad! Say that you will marry your Bananabelle, or I shall die!

ANNABELLE: *(outraged)* WHAT'S THIS?!

*(**Felicity** whirls around. **Elizabeth** gasps.)*

ANNABELLE: *(snatches hat)* Very amusing. So this is what you and your rude little shop-keeper friend do, Bitsy!

FELICITY: Oh, Annabelle! It was only a bit of fun.

ANNABELLE: *(angrily)* Fun? You have no manners! When Mama hears about this she'll tell Bitsy never to speak to you again! You horrible colonial brat! You…

(***Annabelle*** *stops suddenly because* ***Miss Manderly*** *ENTERS and puts the tea tray on the table.* ***Annabelle*** *hangs up her hat, and then flounces over to her chair and sits.)*

MISS MANDERLY: Young ladies, the time has come for you to take turns serving the tea. Annabelle, you are the eldest. You shall serve the tea today.

(***Annabelle*** *sits up very straight, acting important.* ***Felicity, Elizabeth,*** *and* ***Miss Manderly*** *sit down too. After* ***Annabelle*** *prepares the tea, she fills Miss Manderly's cup first, then Elizabeth's cup, and then her own.)*

MISS MANDERLY: Annabelle, my dear. You have forgotten to serve Miss Merriman.

ANNABELLE: *(smugly)* Oh! I was only thinking of the carpet.

MISS MANDERLY: The carpet?

ANNABELLE: Yes, indeed. I did not serve her because I did not want her to toss out the tea all over your fine carpet.

MISS MANDERLY: *(scolding)* Annabelle! Apologize at once!

ANNABELLE: Oh, but Felicity would be proud to toss out her tea. Her father said it is right to toss out tea. He said those hotheads in Yorktown were right to throw the tea into the river.

FELICITY: No! My father did not say that…

ANNABELLE: *(in a mean voice)* Yes, he did! Bitsy heard him in your store yesterday. Didn't you, Bitsy?

(***Elizabeth*** *says nothing.)*

FELICITY: But that's not what he said! Tell her, Elizabeth!

(***Elizabeth*** *won't look at Felicity.)*

FELICITY: My father said the men who threw the tea into the river *thought* they were right. They did it to show the king that they did not agree with the tax on tea.

ANNABELLE: Your *father* disagrees with the king's tax, too! That's why he's not going to sell tea in his store anymore. He is disloyal to the king. Your father is a traitor!

FELICITY: *(angrily)* No! My father is not a traitor! How can you say that? *(She turns to Elizabeth.)* How can you let her say such an awful thing, Elizabeth? You know it isn't true! My father is not a traitor—you are! You are a traitor to me!

(***Felicity*** *grabs her sampler and EXITS, running out of the room.)*

ACT FOUR

Scene: The Merrimans' store, immediately after Act Three.

(***Felicity*** *ENTERS, crying. She is carrying her sampler.* ***Father*** *ENTERS.)*

FATHER: Felicity? *(worried)* What is it, child? What is the matter? *(He starts to cross the room toward her.)*

FELICITY: *(running to him)* Elizabeth and Annabelle think you are a traitor. I don't want to speak to them ever again!

FATHER: Ahhh. It's because of the argument about not selling tea in the store, isn't it?

FELICITY: Aye.

FATHER: My poor child. *(pauses)* I fear there is more of this trouble coming. This talk against the king will cause much sorrow before it is over. It will divide families and destroy friendships, if we let it. *(Gently, he takes Felicity's sampler from her hands.)*

FELICITY: Throw that sampler away! I hate it. It is full of mistakes.

FATHER: *(smoothing out the sampler)* There's a great deal that's good in this sampler. It would be a terrible waste to throw it away just because of a mistake or two. And I think it would be a terrible waste to throw away your friendship with Elizabeth just because of one misunderstanding.

FELICITY: She's not my friend! If she were my friend, she wouldn't have let Annabelle say such awful things!

FATHER: I see. You are afraid Elizabeth does not like you anymore. Is that it?

FELICITY: *(nods sadly)* Aye.

FATHER: I think you are wrong about that. But you will have to go back to your lessons to find out.

FELICITY: *(stubbornly)* I don't want to go to the lessons anymore! I want to forget everything I learned.

FATHER: Aye. *(holding up the sampler)* It is easiest to throw everything away. It is harder to untangle knots and try again. That takes courage.

FELICITY: *(slowly)* What if I do go back? What shall I do when they serve tea? I want to be loyal to you. I don't want to drink tea anymore. *(pause)* But if I am rude, Miss Manderly won't want me to come back ever again. Elizabeth won't want to be my friend. And Annabelle will think she is right, that colonists are uncivilized. *(Felicity looks at her father.)* What shall I do?

FATHER: Now that *is* a difficult knot to untangle. You must be polite, but do what you think is right. I trust you will find a way. *(smiling)* You have become quite a gracious young lady these past few weeks.

*(**Father** kisses Felicity's forehead and EXITS.)*

ACT FIVE

Scene: Miss Manderly's parlor, the next day. Annabelle and Elizabeth are seated at the tea table working on their samplers as Miss Manderly looks on.

*(**Felicity** ENTERS.)*

MISS MANDERLY: Good day, Miss Merriman. I am very glad to see you today.

FELICITY: *(sitting down, taking out her sampler)* Thank you, Miss Manderly.

MISS MANDERLY: *(examining Felicity's work)* Why, Felicity, what fine work! You have untangled all the knots on your sampler.

ELIZABETH: *(bursts out)* Oh, Lissie! Annabelle twisted everything around. *(leaning toward Felicity)* I never said your father was a traitor. Annabelle said that, and I am so sorry I didn't stop her! I was afraid, but I won't be afraid anymore, I…

ANNABELLE: *(rises)* Bitsy! Stop that, Bitsy!

ELIZABETH: *(whirls around in her chair to face Annabelle)* I hate being called Bitsy! From now on, call me *Elizabeth.*

ANNABELLE: Why Bitsy, I...

ELIZABETH: Or I will call you Bananabelle in front of everyone. Annabelle Bananabelle.

*(**Annabelle** huffs and sits down again, fiercely attacking her sampler to hide her anger. **Felicity** smiles at Elizabeth and squeezes her hand.)*

MISS MANDERLY: *(smiling)* Well, Elizabeth. Will you do us the honor of serving tea this afternoon?

*(**Felicity, Elizabeth,** and **Annabelle** set aside their samplers.)*

ELIZABETH: Yes, indeed!

*(**Elizabeth** pours Miss Manderly's tea, then Annabelle's. Before she can fill Felicity's cup, **Felicity** takes a deep breath and, in a graceful gesture that the audience can clearly see, turns her teacup upside down on the saucer and puts her spoon across it.)*

FELICITY: *(politely)* Thank you, Elizabeth. I shall take no tea.

MISS MANDERLY: *(smiling)* Well done, Felicity! Very well done, indeed!

*(**Felicity** sighs with relief as she proudly takes a cake from the tray.)*

Tea for Felicity

A Play About Felicity

Putting on the Play

CONTENTS

PLAY SUMMARY

Tea for Felicity takes place in the fall of 1774, in Williamsburg, the capital of the colony of Virginia. Felicity Merriman is a nine-year-old girl who has just begun taking lessons from Miss Manderly, a gentlewoman who teaches young ladies fine stitchery and the proper way to serve tea. At Miss Manderly's house, Felicity meets Elizabeth and her older sister Annabelle, who have recently arrived from England. Felicity and Elizabeth quickly become good friends.

But changes are in the air. To protest the rule of King George of England, Felicity's father refuses to buy or drink tea, or to sell it in his store. Elizabeth's family supports the rule of the king. Felicity must find a way to remain loyal to her father yet continue her friendship with Elizabeth and the lessons she has come to love.

FELICITY ❦ 1774

In 1774, many American colonists were struggling for independence from England. Felicity was struggling for independence, too—while trying to remain loyal to her family and friends.

THE CHARACTERS

HOW TO BECOME YOUR CHARACTER

Close your eyes and imagine that you are your character. Then practice walking, talking, and moving as you think your character would.

Your imagination is your best tool for a successful performance. If you don't have a stage or elaborate costumes or props, act as if you do!

FELICITY ELIZABETH

MISS MANDERLY

To prepare for your role, study your character description. Check the script to see what other characters say about or to your character. Use those statements as clues to how you should act.

Felicity is a spunky nine-year-old girl. Felicity speaks enthusiastically, and her movements are quick—too quick, at times, to be ladylike. She is torn between her duty to her parents and her own growing need for independence.

Elizabeth is a shy nine-year-old from an English family. She wants to be a good friend to Felicity, but she's afraid of her sister Annabelle. At the beginning of the play, she looks away whenever Annabelle speaks, but by the end, she looks Annabelle in the eye.

Miss Manderly is a gentlewoman who gives lessons in ladylike behavior. She has excellent posture and a ready smile. She is warm and loving to the girls, but she won't put up with rudeness.

Annabelle is Elizabeth's snobby older sister. She bosses Elizabeth and Felicity in private and acts sweet to them when Miss Manderly is nearby. She speaks in a loud, smug voice, as if she would drown out anyone else who might want to talk.

Father is Felicity's father, who owns one of the finest stores in Williamsburg. Father believes that people should do what they feel is right, even if it seems wrong to others. He is loving to Felicity and understands that she must find her own answers.

The Angry Man is upset with Father and the other colonists who want independence. He speaks in an angry voice, and doesn't really listen to Father or anyone else.

Four actors can put on *Tea for Felicity* if one actor takes the parts of Annabelle and Father and another takes the parts of Miss Manderly and the Angry Man.

ANNABELLE

FATHER ANGRY MAN

IF YOU FORGET YOUR LINES . . .

If you forget your lines and can't hear the prompter, just think about what your character would say and then ***ad-lib*** *(say it in your own words).*

THE DIRECTOR

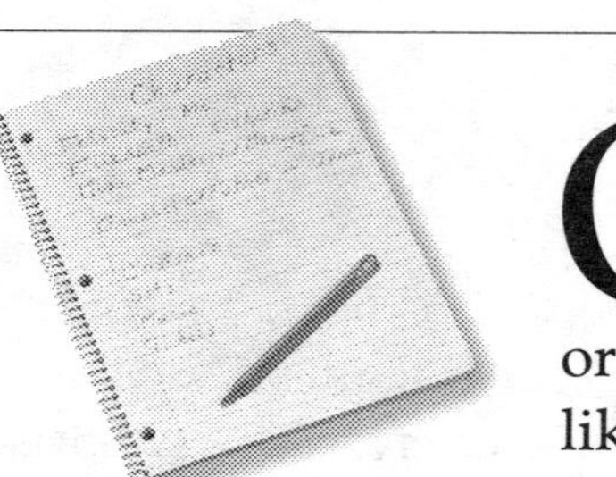

PRAISING THE ACTORS

One of your most important jobs as director is to praise the actors. Watch for good things that happen during rehearsals and make them part of the finished performance. The best praise is specific and sincere. Keep a notebook handy for your notes about things to remember and praise.

One of the director's jobs is to help an actor "get into character" by helping him or her imagine what it would be like to truly be that character. How would a character show joy or anger? For example, would one character show joy by laughing aloud while another smiled quietly? Would a character stamp her foot in anger or turn her back?

Encourage the actors to practice walking and talking as their characters. How would the main character of the play walk? How would her voice change when she is happy or upset? Helping the actors find answers to these kinds of questions will create a more believable performance.

BLOCKING THE ACTION

As the director, you help the actors plan how to move when they're onstage. This is called *blocking the action,* and it usually takes place during rehearsal. The script sometimes tells the actors

how and when to move, but it is your job to give additional directions. You also give the actors little signs, or *cues,* about when to go onstage and offstage.

When you are blocking the action, try to use the whole stage. Important action should take place near the front of the stage, close to the audience.

Actors should face the audience most of the time when they're speaking, so the audience can see the actors' faces and hear their lines. But sometimes you might ask an actor to turn away to show sadness or rejection.

KEEPING THE PLAY MOVING

Keep the play moving by helping the actors *overlap* their lines. To overlap, an actor says her first word just as the actor before says her last word. Combine overlapping with occasional pauses to make the play more lively and natural.

DIRECTOR'S TIPS

- *Make sure that all actors speak clearly and loudly enough to be heard.*
- *Help the actors "get into character" by asking questions about what their characters are like.*
- *Remind the actors to relax as they say their lines. Using props will help them move naturally.*
- *Plan the action so that the audience can see the actors' faces.*
- *Remind the actors not to stand between other actors and the audience.*

THE CREW

MUSIC AND MOOD

Before the show and during set changes and intermissions, set the mood with harpsichord or lute music from the 1700s. Your librarian should be able to help you find the right music.

*Just before the play starts, the stagehand in charge of music can **fade out** the music by gradually lowering the volume until it can no longer be heard.*

Plays are exciting because lots of people work together to make them happen. The people behind the scenes are known as *the crew*. Crew members may include stagehands, costume makers, makeup and hair stylists, ushers, and a prompter.

Stagehands create sets by finding, building, and painting scenery. They also change the scenery between acts and operate the curtain.

The *sound crew* creates sound effects and operates the sound system.

The *lights crew* operates the lighting system.

The *stage manager* works closely with the director to manage what happens onstage. He or she marks the script with every sound or light cue and all set changes, and then makes sure every cue comes on time.

The *property master* or *property mistress* is responsible for finding or making properties—or *props*—and for having the props ready at the right time and in the right place. That way, the actors have exactly what they need each time they go onstage.

Costume makers help the actors find or make costumes. *Makeup* and *hair stylists* help the actors put on makeup and style their hair or wigs.

The *prompter* follows the play line by line in a script book and whispers lines from offstage if an actor forgets them.

Ushers take tickets and lead the audience to their seats. They are sometimes in charge of getting playbills, programs, and tickets ready for the show.

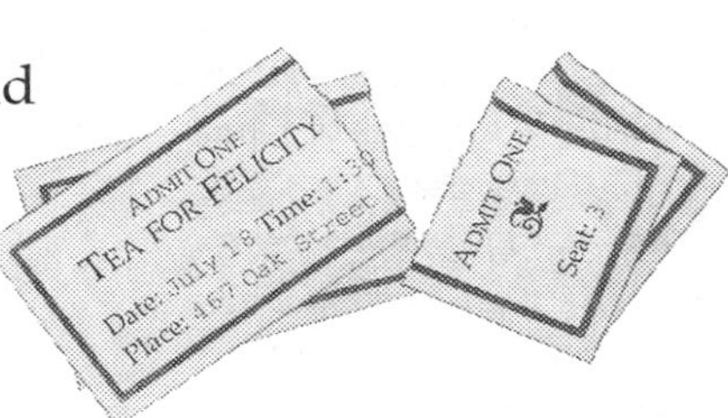

At the end of the performance, everyone who helped put on the show should take a bow at the curtain call!

THE COSTUMES

Costumes help bring a play to life and identify characters—but you can have a great performance without costumes, too!

Felicity wears a long-sleeved jacket, a long skirt, white stockings, black shoes, and a white mob cap. Her hair is tied back with a ribbon in a low ponytail. She wears a wide-brimmed straw hat that goes over her mob cap when she is outside.

Elizabeth wears a long-sleeved gown, white stockings, and black shoes. Her hair is also pulled back in a low ponytail that is tied with a ribbon, and she can wear a pinner cap or a mob cap.

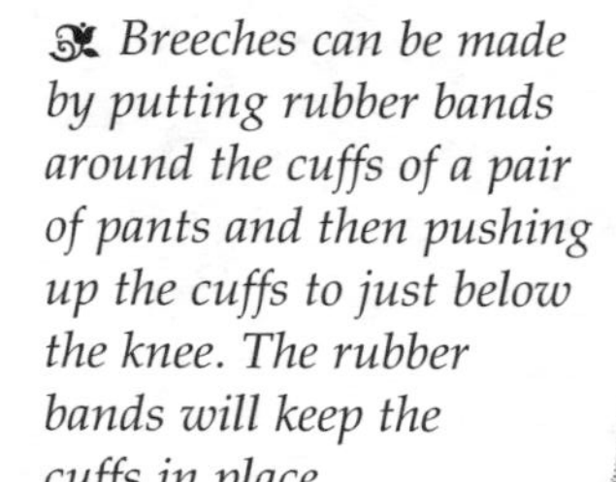

Miss Manderly's clothes are the same style as Elizabeth's but with a lower neckline. Her hair is pinned up in the back and she wears a pinner cap.

COSTUME TIPS

The very simplest way to identify characters doesn't even require costumes! An actor can wear a sign around his or her neck with the character's name printed large enough for the audience to read. This way, actors can easily switch parts without having to switch costumes!

Breeches can be made by putting rubber bands around the cuffs of a pair of pants and then pushing up the cuffs to just below the knee. The rubber bands will keep the cuffs in place.

Annabelle's clothes are fancier than Felicity's or Elizabeth's. Her gown might be made of satin or another fancy material. Instead of a mob cap, she wears a pinner cap similar to Miss Manderly's.

Father wears a long-sleeved white shirt, a vest, a jacket, knee breeches, white stockings, and black shoes. He may have a three-cornered hat that he removes when he is inside.

The Angry Man's clothes are the same style as Father's, but he does not remove his three-cornered hat in the store.

QUICK CHANGES

Practice making quick costume changes. An actor playing both Annabelle and Father has to change costumes four times, so it's important to be able to do so quickly! Quick changes will be easier if costumes are always left in the same place backstage.

In Acts One, Three, and Five, when playing Annabelle, the actor can wear Father's breeches under Annabelle's gown. For Acts Two and Four, the actor should quickly remove the gown and pinner cap and put on Father's vest and jacket.

An actor playing both Miss Manderly and the Angry Man can also wear breeches under the gown.

STAGE SETS

There are two sets needed for *Tea for Felicity*—Miss Manderly's parlor and the Merriman store.

One way to create a background for your set is by using large paper to make a mural. Light-brown paper across the back of your stage works best. You can make two separate murals—one for the parlor and one for the store—or you can make just one mural and use two sets of cutouts. If you pin or lightly tape cutouts to the mural, you can easily change them between acts. For instance, you can make a cutout fireplace by drawing a fireplace on another piece of paper or cardboard and attaching it to the mural. Use paint or chalk to add details to the cutouts and mural. Applying paint with a large sponge is fast and adds texture. Make a mirror or portraits to hang on Miss Manderly's wall by cutting oval frames out of brown construction paper. The center of the mirror can be a sheet of tinfoil, and the portraits can be pictures you've drawn yourself.

Miss Manderly's parlor.

The Merriman store.

Make the store counter out of a large cardboard box (such as a refrigerator box) set on its side. You can also make a counter by draping a dark blanket or sheet over an ironing board or several chair backs. On the mural behind the counter you can draw shelves filled with goods, such as bolts of fabric and glass jars containing cooking supplies.

LIGHTING

Both of the sets are indoor sets, so the lighting should be bright enough so that your audience can see everything clearly, but not so bright that it appears as if the actors are outdoors.

SCENES

ACT ONE
Miss Manderly's parlor

•

ACT TWO
The Merriman store

•

ACT THREE
Miss Manderly's parlor

•

ACT FOUR
The Merriman store

•

ACT FIVE
Miss Manderly's parlor

Props

Props

ACT ONE
A tea set
A silver tea tray
Silverware
Biscuits & cakes

ACT TWO
Felicity's sampler & hoop
A petition

ACT THREE
Elizabeth's sampler & hoop
A tea set
A silver tea tray
Silverware
Annabelle's hat

ACT FOUR
Felicity's sampler & hoop

ACT FIVE
Both samplers & hoops
A tea set

Use a toy tea set, so that when Felicity loses her tooth and the cups go flying, nothing gets broken. Make a tea tray by cutting out a large circle or rectangle of cardboard and covering it with tinfoil so it looks like silver. Or use a plastic tray covered in foil. For biscuits and cakes, use cookies or crackers on a plate.

A *sampler* is a piece of fabric with embroidered letters or shapes stitched on it. The samplers can be scraps of light-colored material. Use a marker to draw a design on each one. Borrow embroidery hoops from someone who does stitchery or buy them at a craft or variety store.

A *petition* is a piece of paper signed by many people. Find a long piece of plain white paper and write lots of names on it so that they look like old-time signatures.

The Stage

There are special terms to describe the front, back, and sides of the stage. These terms were used by actors and directors long ago, and are still used today.

Stages used to be built on a slant, with the back part of the stage higher than the front. This angle allowed the audience to see the actors better. The terms *upstage* and *downstage* come from the way the stage slanted. *Upstage* is the area farthest from the audience—the area that used to be higher. *Downstage* is the front of the stage, nearest the audience. An actor standing in the exact middle of the stage is at *center stage.*

When an actor stands at center stage, facing the audience, the area to the actor's right is *stage right* and the area to the actor's left is *stage left*. The best way to remember *stage right* and *stage left* is to face the audience.

MOB CAPS AND PINNER CAPS

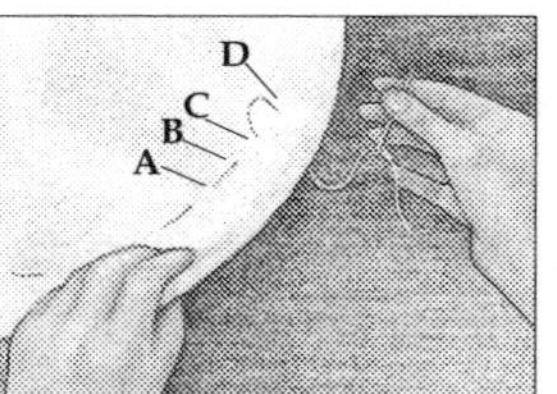

MOB CAP *Step 1*
To sew a running stitch, come up at A and go down again at B. Come up at C and go down again at D.

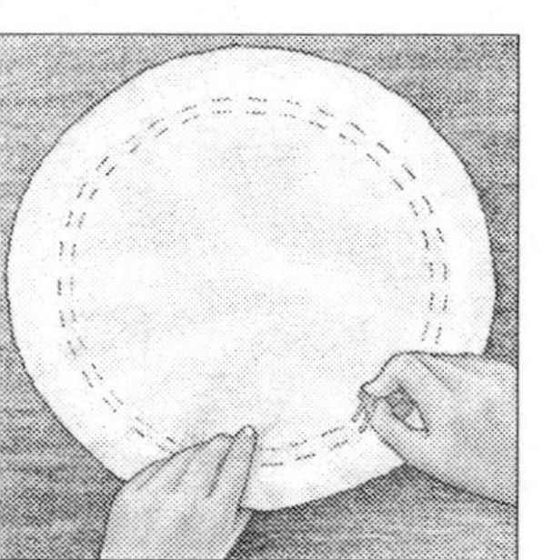

Step 2

Step 3

MOB CAPS

To make a mob cap, use a compass to draw an 18-inch circle on a large piece of paper. Cut out the circle pattern, pin it to a piece of white fabric, and then cut out a fabric circle. Unpin the paper pattern. Knot one end of a long piece of thread and sew a running stitch around the circle, 2 inches in from the edge (see Step 1). When you finish, cut the thread, leaving about 2 inches of loose thread at the end. Knot another long piece of thread and sew a second circle of running stitches 1/4 inch inside the first circle of stitches. Don't cut this thread yet!

Hold the loose threads of both rows by the unknotted ends (see Step 2). Gently pull the two rows of thread until the cap is gathered enough to fit loosely on your head. Tie the threads off so the cap stays gathered. Cut off the excess thread. Finish the cap by sewing on a pretty bow (see Step 3).

PINNER CAPS

To make a pinner cap, use a compass to draw a 4-inch circle on a piece of paper. Cut out the paper circle and pin it on a piece of light cotton fabric. Then cut out the fabric circle. Unpin the paper pattern. Next you'll need 5/8 yard of flat lace or 1/2 yard of pre-gathered lace that is 2 inches wide. Pin the lace around the circle, gathering it gently as you pin. Use a running stitch (see Step 1, at left) to sew the lace around the edge of the circle. When you come back to the place where you started, tie a knot and cut off the extra thread. Remove the pins. Use hairpins to attach the pinner cap to your head.

PINNER CAP
Use a running stitch to sew the lace to the fabric circle.

Home Is Where the Heart Is

Immigration to America—1854

Kirsten ❤ 1854

Kirsten's story is one shared by many of the immigrants who have come to settle in America. It's the story of a dramatic journey, filled with hardships and hope.

About the Play

Home Is Where the Heart Is is a play about Kirsten Larson, a fictional nine-year-old Swedish immigrant arriving in America in 1854.

In the mid-1800s, many Europeans left their homes in search of a better life in America. Many of these early immigrants came from countries where land was expensive or scarce, or farmland was poor. They often came to America with few possessions, looking for a new and better life. Most immigrants could take only what would fit in a few large trunks, or what they could carry on their backs.

In *Home Is Where the Heart Is*, Kirsten and her parents have just arrived in New York after a long sea voyage from Sweden. They are going to join Kirsten's uncle and his new family on a frontier farm in Minnesota. Kirsten is homesick for Sweden and for her grandmother. But becoming best friends with Marta, another Swedish girl on the ship, helps Kirsten feel less lonely.

Now the Larsons must travel halfway across America on the final leg of their journey. Kirsten is excited about traveling on a train for the first time, but is sad to say good-bye again—this time to Marta. When Kirsten and Marta meet again in Chicago, Kirsten is overjoyed. She starts to feel hopeful about her new life, knowing that Marta will be in Minnesota, too. But just before they reach Minnesota, Marta becomes ill with cholera and dies. Kirsten is devastated.

Kirsten and her parents reach Minnesota safely, but they have run out of money. On the dreary walk to Uncle Olaf's farm, Kirsten feels that she will never have another friend and never feel at home in America. Luckily, upon arriving, Kirsten's new cousins make her feel welcome and at home once again.

The story of the Larsons' journey is one shared by many immigrants. In fact, the story of immigration is central to American history. Most Americans have ancestors or more recent family members who came from someplace else. And like Kirsten, many came as children. In *Home Is Where the Heart Is*, Kirsten must find a way to accept the losses she has experienced and to feel at home in a new place. Reading and dramatizing this play will help your students understand what that experience was like. The related activity will help your students experience for themselves some of the feelings—of hope, fear, and loss—that immigrants have felt and continue to feel even today as they arrive in America.

Historical Context

In the 1850s, passenger ships could sail across the Atlantic Ocean in about six weeks. If the wind was bad, the trip could take much longer. Many passengers experienced seasickness, even in good weather. Some died in shipwrecks or in storms at sea. Diseases such as cholera spread fast on ships, and many people died during the crossing or after arriving.

Food spoiled quickly without refrigeration. Bread became moldy, vegetables and fruit rotted, and even salted meat became rotten before reaching land. Still, passengers ate this food because it was all they had. By the time they arrived in America, many immigrants were weak from lack of fresh food.

The dangers of the trip did not end upon reaching America. Most immigrants could not speak English. It was not uncommon for immigrants to be robbed or cheated as they tried to buy tickets for the rest of their journey. But in spite of these challenges and very real dangers, immigrants continued to come, searching for land of their own and a better life.

America's westward expansion in the 1840s and 1850s made it possible for arriving immigrants to have land. The Mexican War and the acquisition of the Oregon Territory had almost doubled the size of the nation. By 1853, the United States was the size and shape it is today, excluding Alaska and Hawaii. But because of the drive westward, American Indians suffered, forced time and again to leave their lands. By 1854, the Sioux and

Immigration Yesterday and Today

In 1850, approximately 370,000 immigrants from all over the world came to America. The population then was about 23 million. Immigration peaked in 1907, when 1,285,000 people arrived and settled into the existing population of 87,000,000 people. In the 1990s, about 1 million immigrants arrive each year, and the U.S. population is over 250 million.

Arriving in America

When Kirsten and her family came to America in 1854, they were able to walk off the boat and right into New York City. At that time, there were few limits to immigration to the United States—usually only health-related. But by the 1890s—when Ellis Island opened in New York Harbor—America's immigrant population had increased dramatically, and limits based on nationality, politics, and health were enforced. Many immigrants who arrived on the West Coast came through San Francisco or Long Beach. Angel Island was opened in 1912 to handle West Coast immigration.

Today, most people immigrating to the United States arrive by air.

Chippewa, who originally inhabited much of what is today Minnesota, had ceded most of the territory to the United States.

Settlers like Kirsten's Uncle Olaf sent letters to their relatives back home telling of the good land and the many opportunities. By 1858, when Minnesota achieved statehood, the land was dotted with a growing number of pioneer farms and the rural communities that served them.

Themes in the Play

Home Is Where the Heart Is could be used very effectively in social studies or history units on immigration and pioneer times. The play could also be used in thematic units about home, loss, belonging, friendship, family, death, and change.

Packing for a Journey

Objectives:
To attribute value to material and sentimental objects

To make difficult choices based on personal values

To pantomime packing, noting the size and weight of objects

Teacher's Role: *Facilitator, or in role as the captain of the spaceship*

Student Roles: *Students play themselves in imaginary circumstances*

Time Needed: *30 minutes*

Space Needed: *A large open space*

Materials Needed: *A suitcase or box*

Preparing to Perform—Packing for a Journey

This activity may be most effective before reading or performing *Home Is Where the Heart Is*. It will help students think about what leaving one's home would be like, and deepen students' understanding of how Kirsten and her family must have felt when they were deciding what to take to America and what to leave behind.

Context

Packing for a journey involves many choices. These decisions are considerably more difficult if you will not be returning. This was Kirsten's predicament when she left Sweden. To experience a similar predicament, your students will pantomime that they are packing for a journey to outer space, from which they will not return. What will they decide is too valuable to leave behind?

Directions

1. The packing: You may go into role as the spaceship captain, or remain out of role to explain the following situation and task: Owing to overpopulation and a lack of food, jobs, and housing, most of the earth's population is being transported by spacecraft to other planets. Everyone in this classroom has been assigned to spaceship Alpha-Omega, which will leave earth tomorrow at 0600 hours. Each passenger is allowed only one suitcase or box with personal belongings. Each suitcase may be no larger than the sample suitcase that will remain in the center of the room so that each traveler can be sure that his or her suitcase is the correct size.

2. The pantomime: Come out of role. Ask students to close their eyes and silently visualize their bedrooms at home. What would they take with them from their bedroom? What might be too big to fit into the suitcase? What will be left behind? When you have finished speaking, the students should silently go to a space in the room and pantomime packing their suitcase. Tell them that they should think about what they want to bring, why they should bring it, and how they're going to pack it so that it is protected during the journey. Give them a minute or two to think about what they want to bring, and then ask them to start their pantomime. Allow students about three to five minutes to pantomime the packing.

3. Lift-off and sharing: As students finish their pantomimed packing, go back into your role and remind everyone that this is the last boarding call for Alpha-Omega. Students should board the spacecraft immediately, taking their luggage with them. As the captain, greet the passengers individually as they board the craft. Ask the student travelers to form a circle in the center of the spaceship. Then ask each traveler to open his or her imaginary suitcase and share with the group what he or she has packed. End the improvisation with questions. How did they choose what to bring? What did they leave behind that they really wanted to take, but couldn't? How did they decide? Did anyone change his or her mind about what to bring after packing? Are suitcases filled mostly with sentimental objects or functional ones? Did anyone pack in a special way, such as wrapping a toothbrush in a special handkerchief embroidered by one's grandmother? The sharing and questioning will probably take about 20 minutes.

4. Revisiting: Consider returning to this activity for more discussion after your students have read and performed the play. Knowing what they know of Kirsten's journey, would they choose differently now?

LUGGAGE

Most immigrants—especially those traveling in steerage—arrived in America with few possessions and without luggage as we know it today. People packed their possessions in cloth bundles, wicker baskets, and small leather satchels or suitcases. Larger trunks were usually made of leather or wood. The wooden trunk that held most of the Larsons' possessions was hand-painted with traditional Swedish patterns.

AN ALTERNATIVE

Ask students to pack for the journey actually using their backpacks rather than imaginary suitcases. Students could pack some practical things, such as shoes, a jacket or sweatshirt, and a pair of jeans, and then see how much room is left in their backpacks. What else would they pack, and why? Then ask them to think about what food they might bring and where and how they would store it.

Home Is Where the Heart Is

A Play About Kirsten

❤

Play Script

TIPS FOR ACTORS

- Use your imagination. If you don't have a fancy stage or elaborate props and costumes, act as if you do!

- Speak clearly and loudly enough to be heard. Don't turn your back to the audience or stand between another actor and the audience.

- Pretend that you **are** the character you are playing. If you forget your lines and can't hear the prompter, think about what the character would really say and say it in your own words.

- Act and speak at the same time. Directions before your lines will tell you things to do as you are saying those lines. For example,

  *(**Kirsten** sways a little.)*

  KIRSTEN: Yes! But Marta, does the land seem to be moving under your feet?

- Other directions make suggestions about how to say a line. For example,

  MARTA: *(whispering)* Kirsten?

- Cooperate with the director and the other actors. And don't forget to smile at the curtain call!

HOME IS WHERE THE HEART IS

A Play About Kirsten

CHARACTERS

KIRSTEN

A nine-year-old Swedish immigrant who is starting a new life in America

MARTA

Kirsten's best friend, who becomes ill on their journey

MAMA

Kirsten's mother, who worries about keeping her family safe on their journey

PAPA

Kirsten's father, who is leading his family to their new home

LISBETH

Kirsten's American cousin, who is eleven years old

ANNA

Lisbeth's younger sister, who is seven years old

The action takes place in the summer of 1854, on a journey from Sweden to Minnesota.

1

ACT ONE

Scene: A park near the docks in New York City.

*(**Kirsten** and **Marta** ENTER. Each girl holds a doll and carries a small bundle. They look around curiously.)*

KIRSTEN: America! *(excitedly)* We're finally here, Marta! In America! I'm so glad to be here at last.

MARTA: I am, too! And I'm glad to get off that ship!

KIRSTEN: Me, too! *(She runs a few steps.)* Just smell the air. Mmm! It's so good to smell land again.

MARTA: *(following)* And to feel land under your feet!

*(**Kirsten** sways a little.)*

KIRSTEN: Yes! But Marta, does the land seem to be moving under your feet?

MARTA: Yes! The ground is spinning around me!

*(**Kirsten** and **Marta** put down their bundles and sit, holding their heads.)*

*(**Mama** ENTERS. She laughs at them kindly. She kneels down between them.)*

MAMA: Do you feel dizzy? Your legs will have to get used to dry land again after three months at sea. *(smiling)* We will have a lot to get used to here in America!

KIRSTEN: Everything in America will be new to us. *(eagerly)* May we go look around the city, Mama?

MAMA: No, Kirsten. You could easily get lost. New York is a big city. Everyone is a stranger and you don't speak English yet. Papa has gone to buy tickets for the rest of our journey to Minnesota. Later you may go with him to buy some bread and milk. We'll wait here in the shade until he gets back.

*(**Kirsten, Marta,** and **Mama** sit on the grass. The girls start to play with their dolls.)*

MARTA: *(after playing a while)* Summer is so hot in America! It's only June, and the grass is already as dry as straw.

KIRSTEN: Yes, it's much hotter than Sweden. *(She fans herself with her hand.)* Even without my quilted petticoats, I'm hot! Will it be this hot in Minnesota, Mama?

MAMA: I don't know, Kirsten. Minnesota is a long way from here. We will have to wait and see.

*(**Papa** ENTERS. He carries a basket full of cherries.)*

PAPA: Kirsten! Mama! Look what I have brought. Cherries!

*(**Papa** stoops down to take cherries from the basket for Mama, Kirsten, and Marta, who eat with great pleasure.)*

MAMA: Oh, I've never seen such huge cherries!

KIRSTEN: Mmm! They're good! And so big!

PAPA: Everything in America is big! Wait until you see the city! And there will be more to see tomorrow. I just bought tickets for our trip to Minnesota. We leave in the morning.

MAMA: *(worried)* Did you find an honest agent? Old Mr. Peterson was cheated of his money by a dishonest agent.

PAPA: *(firmly)* Our agent is a good man. He left Sweden four years ago, and he knows English well. He helped me change our money at a bank.

MAMA: *(sighing)* It's hard, trusting strangers. We are so far from our old home and our old friends. It has been a long, hard journey from Sweden. Now we must go all the way to Minnesota.

PAPA: *(sits near her)* Don't worry. The agent will guide us. He says we will have to travel only a few weeks more. And now that we're on land, it will be easier. We will feel stronger.

KIRSTEN: Don't lose heart, Mama. *(She hugs Mama.)*

MAMA: *(smiling)* No, I won't lose heart now. I know we'll be in our new home soon!

PAPA: *(He stands and helps Mama up.)* Come with me, Mama, and meet the agent and the families we will be traveling with.

*(**Papa** and **Mama** EXIT.)*

*(**Kirsten** and **Marta** continue to eat cherries.)*

KIRSTEN: Papa said we are leaving for Minnesota tomorrow. Are you and your family going tomorrow too, Marta?

MARTA: *(sadly)* Not until the next day.

KIRSTEN: Oh, no! I was so sure our families would be traveling together!

MARTA: Me, too. Are you going to take another ship now?

KIRSTEN: No, I think we are going to take a train to a place called Chicago. *(pauses)* What do you think a train looks like?

MARTA: I don't know exactly. My father says it will make a loud noise and a lot of smoke. We might be afraid of trains.

KIRSTEN: *(grinning)* Noise won't hurt us! Papa says a train is like many wagons all traveling together. Maybe you'll get on our train. Wouldn't that be lucky?

MARTA: Or maybe we won't ever see each other again.

KIRSTEN: *(confidently)* But your family is going to Minnesota, just like mine is. We are sure to meet on the way. At least, I hope so!

MARTA: I hope so, too. *(pauses)* I'll be so lonely without you, Kirsten.

KIRSTEN: *(taking her hand)* I'll be lonely, too. Sometimes I wonder if I'll ever feel at home in America. But I'll tell you what my grandmother said to me when we left Sweden. She said, "When you're lonely, look at the sun. Remember that we all see the same sun."

MARTA: Do you do that? Do you look at the sun and think of your grandmother?

KIRSTEN: Yes. When I'm homesick, I look at the sun and think of her. Then I'm not as homesick anymore.

MARTA: *(with a small smile)* When I get lonely, I'll look at the sun and think of you. But I'll still miss you, Kirsten.

KIRSTEN: I'll miss you too, Marta. But I'll look at the sun and think of you. Then I'll say a prayer. I'll say, "God bless Marta."

MARTA: I'll say a prayer, too. And I'll be looking for you everywhere!

*(From OFFSTAGE, **Mama** calls.)*

MAMA'S VOICE: Kirsten! Kirsten! Come here now!

KIRSTEN: I have to go now. Good-bye, Marta!

*(Both girls stand up. **Kirsten** hugs Marta and holds her doll up for Marta to kiss, then EXITS, running.)*

MARTA: Good-bye, Kirsten! Good-bye!

*(**Marta** waves and EXITS, other side.)*

ACT TWO

Scene: The sunny backyard of a Chicago boarding house.

*(**Kirsten** and **Mama** ENTER. They start to do laundry. They scrub their clothes, hang them on a line, and fold and stack dry things.)*

KIRSTEN: Wasn't the train fast, Mama? It was faster than the fastest horse.

MAMA: Yes, and dirtier than the dirtiest horse, too! Coal grit on the floor and cinders in the air! I'm glad to wash those days and days of soot and smoke out of our clothes. And it was so hot! I thought we would roast on that train!

KIRSTEN: I think our Swedish clothes are too hot for America. *(dreamily)* I wish we could wear pretty dresses like American ladies do. They look so much nicer than our wool skirts and shawls. And cooler, too.

MAMA: Our clothes are clean and sturdy. We don't need to be ashamed of them. Besides, how could I milk cows on Uncle Olav's farm in Minnesota if I wore ruffles?

KIRSTEN: You're right, Mama. Tell me again about Uncle Olav and the farm.

MAMA: Olav left Sweden six years ago, when you were just three. He thought he could make a better life in America. And last year, he wrote to tell us about his new farm. The land is rich and good there, and he needs our help.

KIRSTEN: Now tell the best part. Tell about Uncle Olav's family.

MAMA: *(smiling)* Uncle Olav married Aunt Inger in America. She came from Sweden, too. She was a widow with two daughters about your age. Their names are Anna and Lisbeth.

KIRSTEN: They are my cousins. Do you think we will be friends, Mama?

MAMA: Of course. We'll live on the same farm, and they will be right next door.

KIRSTEN: I hope Marta doesn't live too far away. She will always be my best friend.

*(**Marta** ENTERS. She sneaks up behind Kirsten and taps her on the shoulder.)*

MARTA: Kirsten Larson!

KIRSTEN: Marta! You're here! You're here!

*(**Kirsten** and **Marta** hold hands and whirl around and around. **Mama** smiles at them as she continues working.)*

MARTA: And you're here, too! Oh, I missed you!

KIRSTEN: I missed you, too! But whenever I felt lonely, I looked at the sun and thought about you.

MARTA: I looked at the sun, too! It always made me feel better. But wasn't the train terrible? *(She shakes her head.)* It was so loud and hot and smoky!

KIRSTEN: But it brought us both to Chicago so that we are together again.

MARTA: Yes! Tonight our families will have dinner together and sleep under the same roof. And we are going to walk together from Chicago to the Mississippi River. Then we will be on the same riverboat! My father said that our families will stay together until we land in Minnesota.

KIRSTEN: Oh, that's wonderful! I can't believe our good luck.

MAMA: We are lucky. *(She picks up the folded laundry.)* Come along, girls. I want to talk to Marta's mother. We will plan a special dinner to celebrate being together.

*(**Mama** EXITS with the laundry.)*

KIRSTEN: Tonight we will have clean clothes, good food, a real bed to sleep in, and friends nearby. You know, Marta, I think America may be a good home for us all.

*(**Kirsten** and **Marta** EXIT.)*

ACT THREE

Scene: Evening on the deck of a riverboat.

(***Kirsten*** *ENTERS. She looks out at the water and up at the sky. She seems to be waiting for someone.)*

(***Marta*** *ENTERS. She looks weak and speaks in a hoarse whisper.)*

MARTA: Kirsten!

KIRSTEN: *(She turns and speaks impatiently.) There* you are, Marta! I have been waiting and waiting for you. The sun is going down. I have already counted six fish jumping from the water. And look! See the hawk circling overhead?

MARTA: Yes, I—

(***Marta*** *looks up, then suddenly clutches her stomach and falls to her knees.)*

MARTA: *(groaning)* Oh!...Oh!

KIRSTEN: *(kneeling to help)* Marta! Are you all right? What's the matter? What's wrong? What's wrong?

MARTA: *(slowly, weakly)* I don't... I don't know. I feel terrible. I'm hot, then cold, and my stomach hurts.

KIRSTEN: Oh, Marta! You're shivering!

MARTA: It's so dark, and so cold.

(***Marta*** *shivers and hugs herself.)*

KIRSTEN: Here! I'll put my shawl around you.

MARTA: *(moaning)* Kirsten, I'm so sick.

(***Marta*** *slumps against Kirsten.)*

KIRSTEN: Don't worry, Marta. I'll help you. Lean on me. *(worried)* We've got to get you inside to your mama. Can you stand up? Hold on to me. Slowly, now...

*(**Kirsten** puts Marta's arm over her shoulder and tries to help her stand.)*

MARTA: I…I can't….

*(**Marta** collapses to the ground in a faint.)*

KIRSTEN: *(frightened)* Marta! Marta! Oh, no! Help! Mama, Papa! Help! Help!

*(**Mama** and **Papa** ENTER, looking alarmed.)*

PAPA: What is it? What's happened?

MAMA: What's the matter?

KIRSTEN: *(very scared)* It's Marta! Look! Is she…?

MAMA: *(kneeling over Marta)* She has fainted. Oh, no! The poor child is burning up with fever.

KIRSTEN: But she was shivering before! What's the matter, Mama? What is it? What's wrong with Marta?

*(**Mama** looks sadly at Papa. **Papa** nods.)*

MAMA: Marta is very sick, Kirsten. I think it is cholera. We have to get her to bed.

KIRSTEN: Cholera! No! It can't be! She was fine yesterday!

*(**Papa** hugs Kirsten.)*

PAPA: Calm yourself, Kirsten. Cholera comes on quickly and quickly becomes serious. Mama and I will take care of Marta. We will take her to her parents. You must go—

KIRSTEN: *(breaking in)* No! I have to stay with Marta! I have to!

PAPA: Kirsten, cholera is dangerous. You could get sick, too. Now go. Do as you are told!

KIRSTEN: *(softly, almost crying)* Poor Marta! My poor friend! You must get well. You must!

*(**Mama** and **Papa** EXIT, carrying Marta.)*

*(**Kirsten** EXITS slowly, other side.)*

ACT FOUR

Scene: In the sick bay, just before dawn. Marta is lying on a straw mattress on the floor.

*(**Kirsten** ENTERS. She kneels beside Marta. **Marta** moans and rolls her head from side to side. **Kirsten** smooths the pillow and puts Marta's doll next to her in bed.)*

MARTA: *(whispering)* Kirsten?

KIRSTEN: Yes, I'm here, Marta.

MARTA: You shouldn't be here.

KIRSTEN: I had to see you. Do you feel better?

MARTA: I'm tired. I just feel very tired.

KIRSTEN: Papa says we will get to Minnesota today, Marta. When we get to Minnesota, we will be home. You will feel better.

MARTA: No, I don't think so, Kirsten.

KIRSTEN: Of course you will! You must get well. I will hate Minnesota if you aren't well and we can't play together there. It will never feel like home then.

MARTA: *(slowly, weakly)* You mustn't say that. Home is wherever you have friends. Your cousins will be your friends. They will make you feel at home.

KIRSTEN: *(takes Marta's hand)* But you are my best friend! I'll be so lonely if we are not together!

MARTA: *(looking toward the window)* Look, Kirsten. The sun is coming up.

KIRSTEN: *(nodding)* Yes, I see it.

MARTA: Remember what your grandmother told you? Remember what you and I said about the sun?

KIRSTEN: Whenever I miss you, whenever I am lonely, I should look at the sun and think of you.

MARTA: Remember, we all see the same sun.

KIRSTEN: But Marta...

MARTA: *(whispering)* God bless you, Kirsten.

*(**Marta** dies.)*

KIRSTEN: Marta? Marta! Oh, Marta!

*(**Kirsten** holds Marta's hand to her cheek and cries. **Mama** and **Papa** ENTER. They kneel behind Kirsten.)*

MAMA: Kirsten!

KIRSTEN: She's dead, Mama. Marta is dead.

MAMA: The poor child!

PAPA: God rest her soul.

KIRSTEN: *(sobbing)* Marta, Marta. My friend.

PAPA: *(standing up)* Come, Kirsten. We must go. *(gently helping her up)* The boat has docked. It is time for us to go ashore.

*(**Mama** stands up.)*

KIRSTEN: But what will happen to Marta?

PAPA: *(gently)* The sailors will bury her here. Her soul is in heaven.

KIRSTEN: No, no!

*(**Kirsten** sobs and buries her head in her arms.)*

PAPA: There, there. Enough tears. Stop now, Kirsten.

MAMA: Let her have her tears.

*(**Mama** and **Papa** put their arms around Kirsten. **Kirsten** looks up at the sun.)*

KIRSTEN: *(softly)* God bless you, Marta!

*(**Kirsten, Mama,** and **Papa** EXIT.)*

ACT FIVE

Scene: A rainy afternoon on the road to Uncle Olav's farm.

(Sound effects of rain.)

*(**Papa** and **Mama** ENTER. They are carrying heavy bundles. They are tired. **Papa** brushes rain from his clothes as he looks back over his shoulder.)*

PAPA: Where is Kirsten?

MAMA: She's a little way behind us.

PAPA: Let's stop here and wait for her. It's not raining quite so hard anymore.

MAMA: All right. Let's rest on this rock.

*(**Mama** and **Papa** put their bundles down and sit on the rock.)*

PAPA: Is your bundle heavy, Mama?

MAMA: It *is* too heavy, but that is my own fault. I wanted to bring too many things.

PAPA: I'm sorry we did not have enough money left to rent a horse and wagon.

MAMA: We have our good legs. I don't mind walking. But I am sorry we had to leave the trunks behind. Almost everything we own is in those trunks.

PAPA: It can't be helped. We'll send for the trunks soon. Don't lose heart.

MAMA: I won't. *(sincerely)* People are more important than things. I thank God we are all together and well.

PAPA: *(looking around at the land)* Olav wrote us the truth. The soil here is good. We'll have a better life.

*(**Kirsten** ENTERS, carrying a bundle and looking very sad.)*

MAMA: *(gently)* Kirsten, put your bundle down. Rest for a while.

KIRSTEN: Yes, Mama.

*(**Kirsten** puts her bundle down and sits beside Mama.)*

PAPA: Cheer up, Kirsten. It can't be too much farther to your Uncle Olav's farm. *(standing up)* I'll walk on and ask the way at this farm up ahead.

*(**Papa** EXITS with his bundle.)*

MAMA: Oh, Kirsten, look at you! Your skirt is soaked through to your petticoat. Try to scrape some of the mud off your boots.

KIRSTEN: I wish this rain would stop.

MAMA: The rain will stop soon. And we will be home soon.

KIRSTEN: *(angrily)* Minnesota will never be home for me.

MAMA: Kirsten!

KIRSTEN: *(stubbornly)* It won't! Not without Marta!

MAMA: Oh, my poor Kirsten. *(gently hugging her)* Didn't Marta say, "Home is wherever you have friends"?

KIRSTEN: *(frustrated)* Yes, but I don't have any friends here. Marta was my oldest and best friend. She was my only friend in America. Now she is gone. And there isn't even any sun to look at when I am lonely for her.

MAMA: Old friends are very dear, and we always carry them in our hearts. But we must leave room in our hearts for new friends, too. *(gently but firmly)* Your cousins Anna and Lisbeth will be good friends if you let them, Kirsten. And Uncle Olav and Aunt Inger want to share their farm with us. They want us to make it our home. Promise me you'll try.

KIRSTEN: All right, Mama. I promise.

MAMA: Then I promise you will soon be happy here in Minnesota. *(standing up)* Now we had better catch up with Papa.

*(**Mama** lifts her bundle and starts to walk. As she does, the sun comes out.)*

KIRSTEN: *(calling)* Look, Mama, the sun is coming out!

MAMA: Of course it is. Now come along.

*(**Mama** EXITS.)*

*(**Kirsten** stops to look up at the sun.)*

KIRSTEN: God bless you, Marta! Oh, Marta, I wish you were here to be my friend. But I will try to leave room in my heart for new friends.

*(**Anna** and **Lisbeth** ENTER. Anna is carrying a small bouquet of wildflowers. They call out happy greetings as they run across the stage to Kirsten.)*

ANNA: Hello! Hello!

LISBETH: It's you! At last!

*(**Anna** and **Lisbeth** hug Kirsten.)*

LISBETH: You must be Kirsten! I'm Lisbeth! I've watched for you every single day.

ANNA: *(very excitedly)* I've watched, too! I'm Anna!

LISBETH: Come along and meet our mama and papa. Then we'll show you your cabin.

ANNA: Yes! Come and see your new American home.

LISBETH: Oh, Kirsten, we're so glad you're here! You'll live right next door, and we'll be friends.

*(**Lisbeth** nudges Anna with her elbow to remind her about the flowers.)*

ANNA: Yes! We will all be friends! *(handing flowers to Kirsten)* And these are for you! Welcome home, Kirsten, welcome home!

KIRSTEN: *(smelling the flowers)* Thank you! It's good to be home at last!

*(**Kirsten, Lisbeth,** and **Anna** EXIT happily.)*

Home Is Where the Heart Is

A Play About Kirsten

Putting on the Play

Contents

Play Summary

The play starts as nine-year-old Kirsten Larson and her family arrive in New York in 1854, after a long sea voyage from Sweden. Now they must start their journey to Minnesota, where they will settle on a small farm with Kirsten's uncle and his family. As they travel across the country, Kirsten begins to think she will never feel at home again—especially when her best friend Marta becomes ill on the journey. Happily, Kirsten finds a lot of love waiting for her on a small frontier farm—and learns that home is where the heart is.

Kirsten ❤ 1854

Kirsten's story is one shared by many of the immigrants who have come to settle in America. It's a dramatic journey, filled with hardships and hope.

The Characters

How to Become Your Character

❤ *Close your eyes and imagine that you are your character. Then practice walking, talking, and moving as you think your character would.*

❤ *Your imagination is your best tool for a successful performance. If you don't have a stage or elaborate costumes or props, act as if you do!*

KIRSTEN

MARTA

MAMA

To prepare for your role, study your character description. Check the script to see what other characters say about or to your character. Use those statements as clues to how you should act.

Kirsten is a nine-year-old immigrant just arriving in America. She has bravely left her home in Sweden, but starting over in America scares her a little.

Marta is also nine years old, and is Kirsten's best friend. Marta is quieter and more timid than Kirsten.

Mama is Kirsten's mother. She worries about whether her family will be safe on their long journey, but she never loses heart. She understands when Kirsten is sad, but she knows that pioneers must be strong, too.

PAPA

LISBETH

ANNA

Papa is Kirsten's father. He is a firm, confident, and quiet man. Papa is sometimes gruff but always loving.

Lisbeth is Kirsten's 11-year-old cousin. She lives on the Minnesota frontier and is very excited about having her cousin come to live with her family. Lisbeth and her family left Sweden six years ago.

Anna is Lisbeth's younger sister. She is seven years old and full of love and hope.

Four actors can put on *Home Is Where the Heart Is* if one actor takes the parts of Marta and Anna and another actor takes the parts of Papa and Lisbeth.

If You Forget Your Lines . . .

❤ *If you forget your lines and can't hear the prompter, just think about what your character would say and then* ***ad-lib*** *(say it in your own words).*

The Director

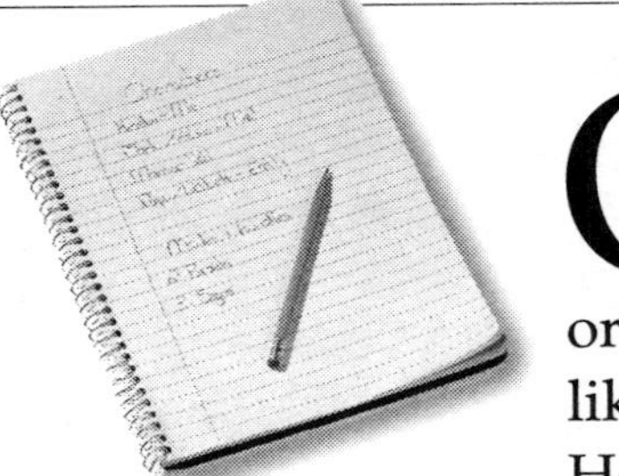

Praising the Actors

- *One of your most important jobs as director is to praise the actors. Watch for good things that happen during rehearsals and make them part of the finished performance. The best praise is specific and sincere. Keep a notebook handy for your notes about things to remember and praise.*

One of the director's jobs is to help an actor "get into character" by helping him or her imagine what it would be like to truly be that character. How would a character show joy or anger? For example, would one character show joy by laughing aloud while another smiled quietly? Would a character stamp her foot in anger or turn her back?

Encourage actors to practice walking and talking as their characters. How would the main character of the play walk? How would her voice change when she is happy or upset? Helping the actors find answers to these kinds of questions will create a more believable performance.

Blocking the Action

As the director, you help the actors plan how to move when they are onstage. This is called *blocking the action*, and it usually takes place during rehearsal. The script sometimes tells the actors

how and when to move, but it is your job to give additional directions. You also give the actors little signs, or *cues*, about when to go onstage and offstage.

When you are blocking the action, try to use the whole stage. Important action should take place near the front of the stage, close to the audience.

Actors should face the audience most of the time when they're speaking, so the audience can see the actors' faces and hear their lines. But sometimes you might ask an actor to turn away to show sadness or rejection.

Keeping the Play Moving

Keep the play moving by helping the actors *overlap* their lines. To overlap, an actor says her first word just as the actor before says her last word. Combine overlapping with occasional pauses to make the play more lively and natural.

Director's Tips

- *Make sure that all actors speak clearly and loudly enough to be heard.*
- *Help the actors "get into character" by asking questions about what their characters are like.*
- *Remind the actors to relax as they say their lines. Using props will help them move naturally.*
- *Plan the action so that the audience can see the actors' faces.*
- *Remind the actors not to stand between other actors and the audience.*

THE CREW

MUSIC AND MOOD

❤ *Before the show and during set changes and intermission, set the mood with Swedish fiddle or accordion music.*

Just before the play starts, the stagehand in charge of music can ***fade out*** *the music by gradually lowering the volume until it can no longer be heard.*

Plays are exciting because lots of people work together to make them happen. The people behind the scenes are known as *the crew*. Crew members may include stagehands, costume makers, makeup and hair stylists, ushers, and a prompter.

Stagehands create sets by finding, building, and painting scenery. They also change the scenery between acts and operate the curtain.

The *sound crew* creates sound effects and operates the sound system.

The *lights crew* operates the lighting system.

The *stage manager* works closely with the director to manage what happens onstage. He or she marks the script with every sound or light cue and all set changes, and then makes sure every cue comes on time.

The *property master* or *property mistress* is responsible for finding or making *properties*—or *props*—and for having the props ready at the right time and in the right place. That way, the actors have exactly what they need each time they go onstage.

Costume makers help the actors find or make costumes. *Makeup* and *hair stylists* help the actors put on makeup and style their hair or wigs.

The *prompter* follows the play line by line in a script book and whispers lines from offstage if an actor forgets them.

Ushers take tickets and lead the audience to their seats. They are sometimes in charge of getting playbills, programs, and tickets ready for the show.

At the end of the performance, everyone who helped put on the show should take a bow at the curtain call!

SOUND EFFECTS

❤ *A member of the sound crew can make the sound of the rain in Act Five with an aluminum pie pan and a cup of uncooked rice. The crew member should drop the grains of rice one at a time into the pan. Practicing will help him or her see how fast to drop the rice to make the rain sound real.*

THE COSTUMES

COSTUME TIPS

- *The very simplest way to identify characters doesn't even require costumes! An actor can wear a sign around his or her neck with the character's name printed large enough for the audience to read. This way, actors can easily switch parts without having to switch costumes!*
- *Costumes in dark colors—black and dark reds, blues, and greens—will look more like immigrants' clothing than light-colored clothing.*
- *A long-sleeved white shirt with the sleeves tied around the waist makes a fine half-apron.*
- *A shawl can be made from a large square or rectangular scarf or even a bath towel.*
- *Lisbeth and Anna can wear scarves tied behind their heads if they don't have sunbonnets.*

Costumes help bring a play to life and identify characters—but you can have a great performance without costumes, too!

Kirsten wears traditional Swedish clothing—a dark, full skirt that ends just above her ankles, a petticoat, a half-apron, a long-sleeved blouse, and a shawl that covers a vest. She also wears boots and long stockings, even though it is summer. Her hair is in two braids that are curled around her ears.

Marta's clothes are the same style as Kirsten's, although they can be another color. Marta's hair is in one braid at the back of her neck.

Mama wears Swedish clothes much like Kirsten's and Marta's. Her head is always covered with a scarf that is tied under her chin.

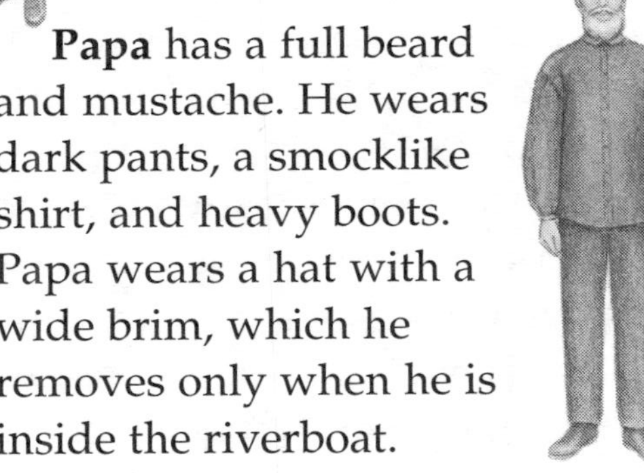

Papa has a full beard and mustache. He wears dark pants, a smocklike shirt, and heavy boots. Papa wears a hat with a wide brim, which he removes only when he is inside the riverboat.

Lisbeth and **Anna** wear simple, one-piece dresses, with long, full skirts. They wear half-aprons, pantalettes, and sunbonnets. Their hair is parted in the middle and braided.

QUICK CHANGES

- *Practice making quick costume changes. An actor who plays both Marta and Anna can wear Anna's dress and apron, covered by Marta's blouse and shawl. When she switches to Anna, she can remove the shawl and blouse and add a sunbonnet or scarf.*
- *An actor playing both Papa and Lisbeth can change quickly by pulling Lisbeth's dress over Papa's costume and rolling up the pants legs. Don't forget to remove Papa's beard and mustache!*
- *Quick changes will be easier if costumes and props are always left in the same place backstage.*

STAGE SETS

SCENES

❤

ACT ONE
A park near the docks on a sunny day in New York City

•

ACT TWO
The sunny backyard of a Chicago boarding house

•

ACT THREE
The deck of a riverboat, at sunset

•

ACT FOUR
In the riverboat's sick bay, just before dawn

•

ACT FIVE
A muddy road on a rainy afternoon

Home Is Where the Heart Is has four outdoor scenes and one indoor scene. You can use the same set for all five acts, but change the way it looks between acts.

One way to create a background is by using large paper to make a mural. Light-brown paper across the back of your stage works best. You can also make cutouts to attach to your background. If you pin or lightly tape cutouts to the mural, you can easily change them from act to act.

Use paint or chalk to add details on the cutouts and the mural. Applying paint with a large sponge is fast and adds texture. Bushes can be cut out and taped on the mural or made from brown paper bags. Crumple the bags slightly and fill them partway with crumpled newspapers. Then paint them lightly with green paint and put several together to create bigger or higher bushes.

LIGHTING

You can use lights to set the mood. It's bright and sunny during Acts One and Two. Act Three takes place at sunset, when it is getting darker. Act Four occurs before sunrise, so it is very dark. Act Five starts when it is dark and rainy, but the sky clears and finally Kirsten sees the sun again. If you don't have a light with a dimmer switch, the stagehand in charge of lights can turn lights on and off as necessary.

ACT ONE
Use large boxes for trunks.

ACT TWO
Use a washtub and a clothesline for the boarding house set.

ACT THREE
Make a ship's railing by using chairs turned with the backs to the audience.

ACT FOUR
Use a rug or towel as a mat on the floor of the sick bay.

ACT FIVE
Use a stool, box, or bench as a rock. Hang a paper sun from the ceiling or a post.

PROPS

PROPS

❤

ACT ONE
Two rag dolls
Two small bundles
A basket of cherries

•

ACT TWO
A pile of laundry
A bucket and washboard
A clothesline
Peg clothespins

•

ACT THREE
Kirsten's rag doll
A shawl

•

ACT FOUR
A mat in the sick bay
A pillow
A blanket

•

ACT FIVE
Three heavy bundles
A small bouquet of flowers

Here are some ideas for making or finding the props for this play.

Use real rag dolls or small stuffed toys for the rag dolls. A *bundle* is a group of objects wrapped together. Make bundles by using a towel, a piece of fabric, or a pillowcase to hold things. Don't make the bundles heavy, or it will be hard for the actors to carry them!

The basket could hold cherries or some other fruit. If you use a fruit other than cherries, be sure to change the script so the actors say the right thing!

Towels or lightweight pieces of fabric can be used for the laundry, shawl, pillow, and blanket. Make a clothesline by tying rope or string between doorways or windows. Or stagehands can stand very quietly onstage, holding up the ends of the rope.

THE STAGE

There are special terms to describe the front, back, and sides of the stage. These terms were used by actors and directors long ago, and are still used today.

Stages used to be built on a slant, with the back part of the stage higher than the front. This angle allowed the audience to see the actors better. The terms *upstage* and *downstage* come from the way the stage slanted. *Upstage* is the area farthest from the audience—the area that used to be higher. *Downstage* is the front of the stage, nearest the audience. An actor standing in the exact middle of the stage is at *center stage.*

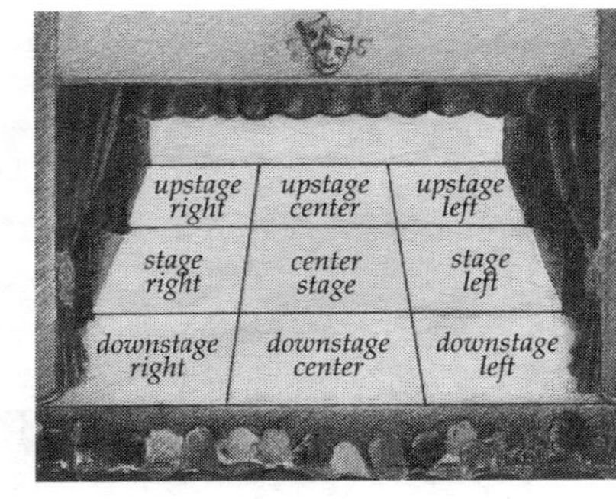

When an actor stands at center stage, facing the audience, the area to the actor's right is *stage right* and the area to the actor's left is *stage left*. The best way to remember *stage right* and *stage left* is to face the audience.

BRAIDS AND BEARDS

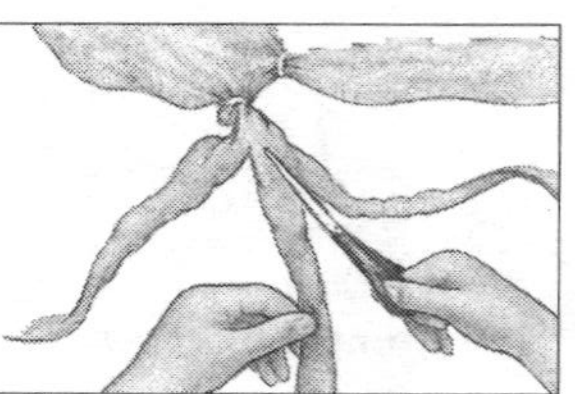

STOCKING BRAIDS
Don't braid too tightly! The braids will look better if they are a little loose.

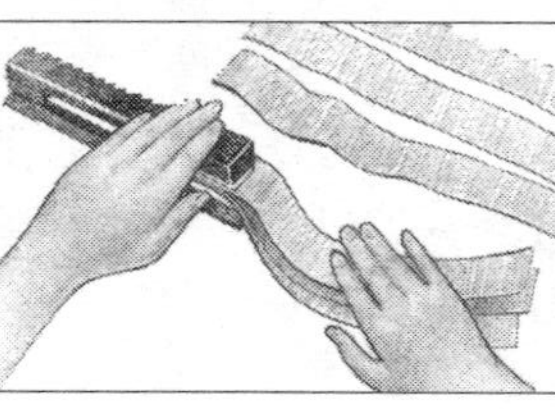

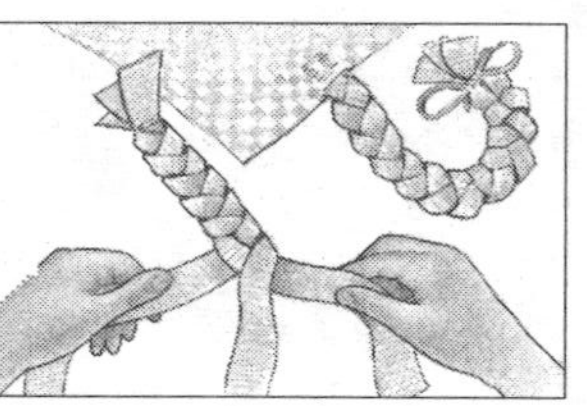

CREPE-PAPER BRAIDS
Attach the braids to the bonnet or scarf with staples or thread.

STOCKING BRAIDS

Use a pair of pantyhose to make braids! Fit the waistband around your head, with the legs hanging down your back. Use small rubber bands to mark where each braid will start. Then take the stockings off your head and—starting at the toe—cut each leg into three long strips, up to the rubber band. Braid each leg and tie the ends with ribbons.

CREPE-PAPER BRAIDS

Braids can also be made from crepe paper. For one braid, cut three long pieces of yellow, tan, or brown crepe paper and staple them together at one end. Then braid the three pieces together. Tie the end of the braid with a ribbon or string. Attach the braid to the back of a scarf or bonnet, or make two braids and attach them to the sides of a bonnet.

A CONSTRUCTION-PAPER BEARD

To make a paper beard, fold a piece of construction paper in half. Use scissors to cut narrow fringes from the bottom almost to the fold. Gently curl the fringes with the scissors as you would curl a ribbon. Punch two small holes at the edges near the fold. Tie a 10-inch piece of string in each hole, and you'll be able to run the string over your ears and tie the beard behind your head.

Papa's mustache could be painted on with an eyebrow pencil. If the same actor plays both Papa and Lisbeth, keep cold cream and tissues on hand to remove the mustache quickly before Lisbeth goes onstage!

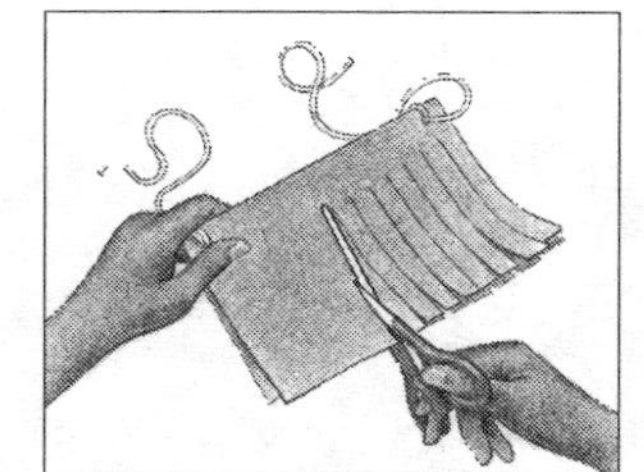

A PAPER BEARD
Be careful not to cut into the fold when making the fringe for Papa's beard.

Program Blackline Master

Program

Home Is Where The Heart Is

A play in five acts about Kirsten Larson, a nine-year-old Swedish immigrant who comes to America in 1854. The play starts as Kirsten and her family arrive in New York. Now they must start another long journey to their new home on the Minnesota frontier.

Starring ________________ *as Kirsten*

________________ *as Marta*

________________ *as Mama*

________________ *as Papa*

________________ *as Lisbeth*

________________ *as Anna*

Director ________________

The crew ________________

____

Date __________ *Time* __________

Place ________________

Sample program

Program

Starring ________________ *as*

________________ *as*

________________ *as*

________________ *as*

________________ *as*

________________ *as*

Director ________________

The crew ________________

____

Date __________ *Time* __________

Place ________________

For a play program, you may photocopy this program master, photocopy and insert a play title and description from page 95, and fill in the names.

Friendship and Freedom

Civil War America—1864

Addy ✹ 1864

Addy's story is one shared by many African Americans who lived during Addy's time. The courage they needed to survive and escape from slavery helped them face the choices and challenges of freedom.

About the Play

Friendship and Freedom is a play about Addy Walker, a fictional nine-year-old girl living in Philadelphia in 1864. Addy and her mother have made a dangerous escape from North Carolina, where they were enslaved, and they are living in freedom for the first time. They are separated from the rest of the family—because of slavery and because of the Civil War.

As *Friendship and Freedom* begins, Addy is about to start school for the first time. Addy has never been to school; it was illegal in most southern states to teach African Americans to read and write. But even in the North, not all African American children were lucky enough to go to school. Many had to work to help their parents earn money so their families could survive. Even in freedom, it was difficult for black people to get good jobs. Black children who did attend school in the North were usually taught in segregated schools that were crowded, had few supplies, and were in poor buildings.

So far, freedom has not been what Addy had expected. She and her mother live in a dark, dreary garret. Her mother works long hours as a seamstress, and Addy hardly ever gets to see her. Worst of all, they don't know where Addy's father, brother, and baby sister are.

But Addy has a new friend, Sarah, whom she met on her first day in Philadelphia. They have quickly become best friends. Sarah is in Addy's class and proudly helps Addy write her name for the first time. When the teacher asks Addy to sit next to Harriet, another girl in their class, Sarah is disappointed. Harriet is a snobby rich girl who makes fun of Sarah because Sarah's family is poor. But Addy is captivated by Harriet, who has all the things that Addy had dreamed freedom would bring her: Harriet is smart, she has pretty clothes, and she lives in a nice house.

Even though Sarah warns Addy about Harriet, Addy is fascinated by her. Although Addy wants to be friends with both Sarah and Harriet, she quickly discovers that that is impossible.

Addy is torn between her loyalty to Sarah, who is poor but honest and loyal, and her attraction to Harriet, who seems to have everything that Addy wants. As Addy adjusts to life in freedom and settles into school, she must struggle with the contradictions, challenges, and choices that come with freedom.

Historical Context

During the 1850s, the conflict over slavery intensified between the North and the South. As the United States grew, the issue of extending slavery in the West was hotly contested, and abolitionists became increasingly vocal. Finally, Abraham Lincoln ran for president on a platform opposed to the spread of slavery. In December 1860, just one month after Lincoln's election, the first southern state seceded from the Union. Eventually eleven southern states left the Union to form the Confederate States of America. The Civil War began officially in April 1861—just weeks after Lincoln took office—when Confederate forces opened fire on Union forces at Fort Sumter in South Carolina.

On January 1, 1863, the Emancipation Proclamation took effect, freeing slaves in the states in rebellion. It was ignored by slave owners, but it gave hope to slaves and abolitionists that the end of slavery was within reach. The Battle of Gettysburg in July 1863 was a major victory for the Union and turned the tide of the war toward the North.

By 1864, when Addy's story takes place, the Civil War was drawing to a close. But the costs of the war were huge, especially to the South. Crops had been destroyed or left untended as the war wore on. The Union's blockade of southern ports made it hard to sell what goods were produced, and high inflation diminished remaining financial reserves. Many landowners needed money to run their plantations and farms—even with slave laborers working the land. As a result, some slave owners sold their slaves in order to get money.

School Supplies

Children in most northern cities, including Philadelphia, went to segregated schools. The schools for black children often were crowded and had few supplies. Books and paper were expensive, so children learned to write on ***slates,*** *made of a soft rock that can be divided into thin layers. Pieces of slate were cut into squares and rectangles, polished smooth, and framed in wood.*

Students used ***slate pencils*** *made of moist slate powder pressed to form sticks that looked like pencils.*

Students in Addy's time sometimes learned math by using an ***abacus.***

Historical Parallels

Addy's family is divided, just as the nation is divided during the Civil War.

When slaves were sold, it usually meant that family members were separated—often never to see each other again. Many African American families were cruelly split apart this way, both before and during the war. It was the sale of Addy's father and brother to another plantation that pushed Addy and her mother to escape: Addy's mother was afraid that the rest of the family would be sold, too, and possibly separated forever.

But life in Philadelphia in 1864 wasn't quite what Addy had expected. Black residents of Philadelphia faced discrimination and prejudice every day. Segregation kept blacks out of many restaurants, hotels, schools, churches, and clubs. Even many of the streetcars were segregated.

The Civil War ended on April 9, 1865, one month after Lincoln's second term began. Less than a week later, Lincoln was shot and killed by actor John Wilkes Booth. But it wasn't until December 18, 1865, that the Thirteenth Amendment to the Constitution was finally ratified, prohibiting slavery throughout the United States and its territories.

Themes in the Play

Friendship and Freedom could be used in a social studies unit on the Civil War, or in thematic units about freedom, slavery, community, education, friendship, loyalty, families, segregation, conflict and conflict resolution, or change.

After Performing—Adult Illiteracy

ADULT ILLITERACY

Objectives:
To problem-solve in a difficult situation

To consider the problems of illiteracy, especially adult illiteracy

To encourage students to be active and thoughtful audience members

To realistically portray the characters of Momma and Mrs. Standards in an improvised scene

Teacher's Role: *Facilitator*

Student Roles: *Some will be performers, most will be audience members*

Time Needed: *25 minutes*

Space Needed: *An open area for the performers, and seats or floor space for the audience*

Materials Needed: *Two chairs for the performers, two index cards, and a VCR remote control (optional)*

This activity, which may be most effective after reading the play, allows students to explore the difficulties faced by people—in this case Addy's mother—who don't know how to read.

Context

Addy can finally attend school and learn to read and write. But Addy's mother has not had that chance. Momma doesn't need to be able to read and write to be the accomplished seamstress that she is. But she does need to do so for other parts of her job, such as making deliveries to Mrs. Ford's customers. When she was hired by Mrs. Ford, Momma didn't tell her that she couldn't read—even when Mrs. Ford told Momma that she would be expected to make some deliveries. Not being able to read cost her her job, and now, as she is looking for a new job, she is faced with the issue again.

Directions

1. Prepare materials: Place two chairs in the front of the room. Write descriptions about Momma and Mrs. Standards on index cards—or copy the descriptions in Appendix B (page 156) and paste them onto the cards.

2. Prepare the scene: The two actors who will be Momma and Mrs. Standards should prepare to act out a job interview, one in which Mrs. Standards asks questions about Momma's skill and experience as a seamstress. Momma should answer these questions clearly and with pride, and Mrs. Standards should act impressed. Tell them to end the scene with the question, "And can you read and write?" Momma should consider, but not respond right away. Warn the actors that you will be starting and stopping their work, as if it were on video, by saying "start," "stop," "rewind," or "fast forward."

3. Share the scene: Explain to the audience that they will be watching a job interview. Ask the performers to briefly describe their characters. Momma should explain how she lost her last job. Then start the scene. After Mrs. Standards says her last line, "And can you read and write?", call out "Stop!" Use a VCR remote control as you do so, or pantomime that you have one.

4. Audience intervention: Once you've stopped the action, ask the audience how Momma should respond. Audience members can suggest various courses of action and the actors could perform them, or an audience member could replace one of the actors. Run through the scene several times, starting with the question that stopped the action and trying various responses and scenarios. What happens if Momma doesn't tell the truth? What happens if she does? If she admits she can't read, will she lose the job? Will she and Addy go hungry? Does Mrs. Standards ever find out Momma's job history? Continue rerunning the scene with changes until the class feels that the best possible solution has been reached.

5. Reflection and discussion: After the scene has been run several times, end the action and discuss Momma's predicament in this interview. If she doesn't tell the truth, will she be comfortable with herself? Might she be found out? Does she need to be able to read to be a good seamstress? Is there a way she can tell the truth and still get the job? How could she learn to read?

ADULT ILLITERACY

Discuss the overall problem of adult illiteracy. What do you need to know to have a job? How important is reading to doing a job well? How do illiterate adults earn a living? Was it different in Momma's time than today? Are there people today who do not know how to read? What other problems might you have if you couldn't read?

Friendship and Freedom

A Play About Addy

Play Script

TIPS FOR ACTORS

- Use your imagination. If you don't have a fancy stage or elaborate props and costumes, act as if you do!

- Speak clearly and loudly enough to be heard. Don't turn your back to the audience or stand between another actor and the audience.

- Pretend that you **are** the character you are playing. If you forget your lines and can't hear the prompter, think about what the character would really say and say it in your own words.

- Act and speak at the same time. Directions before your lines will tell you things to do as you are saying those lines. For example,

  *(**Miss Dunn** pins a medal on Addy.)*

  MISS DUNN: Congratulations, Addy.

- Other directions make suggestions about how to say a line. For example,

  SARAH: *(proudly)* This my Christmas dress from last year.

- Cooperate with the director and the other actors. And don't forget to smile at the curtain call!

FRIENDSHIP AND FREEDOM

A Play About Addy

CHARACTERS

ADDY

A nine-year-old girl who has escaped from slavery with her mother and has a new life in freedom

MOMMA

Addy's mother, who works hard as a seamstress and hopes her family will be reunited in freedom

SARAH

Addy's best friend, who is also nine years old and who is helping Addy learn about life in Philadelphia

MISS DUNN

Addy's kind and helpful teacher

HARRIET

A rich and snobby nine-year-old girl at Addy's school

MAVIS

Harriet's friend, who is also nine years old

The action takes place in the fall of 1864, in Philadelphia.

1

ACT ONE

Scene: The small garret where Addy and her mother live, above the dress shop where Momma works. Momma is standing behind Addy, braiding Addy's hair.

MOMMA: Your poppa'd be proud to see you going off to the first day of school.

ADDY: *(sadly)* I wish we knew where Poppa and Sam are. I miss them and Esther so much.

MOMMA: I do, too. It broke my heart to leave Esther behind. But we couldn't bring her with us. We never would've gotten away from the plantation like we did.

ADDY: They won't sell her like they sold Poppa and Sam, will they?

MOMMA: No, Addy. She's just a baby. And at least we know Esther's safe.

ADDY: When we gonna live together again like a real family?

MOMMA: I don't know, Addy. *(firmly)* But I do know we still a family, even though we ain't all in one place.

ADDY: I wish you didn't have to work so hard. *(pauses)* This ain't the way I dreamed freedom would be. We got to buy everything now—food, candles, coal, matches. And it all cost so much.

MOMMA: Freedom got a cost. It cost money and hard work and heartache. But there ain't nobody here that own us, and beat us, and work us like animals. I got me a paying job. And you can go to school and learn to read and write. *(Momma finishes tying a ribbon on Addy's braids.)*

ADDY: I'm gonna work hard at school, Momma.

MOMMA: *(hugging Addy)* I know you will. You a smart girl.

*(**Sarah** ENTERS, carrying a lunch pail.)*

SARAH: *(excited)* You ready, Addy?

MOMMA: *(smiling)* You look real nice, Sarah.

SARAH: *(proudly)* This my Christmas dress from last year.

ADDY: Do the girls dress real fancy at school?

SARAH: Some do. But don't you worry. *(She crosses the room to Addy.)* You look fine, Addy. You gonna like school. You'll see. *(She takes Addy's hand.)*

ADDY: Wish I could read.

SARAH: Not reading is nothing to be 'shamed about. Our teacher, Miss Dunn, will teach you to read. She taught me. And I can help you learn, too.

ADDY: I'd like that.

SARAH: I'm gonna help you, I promise.

MOMMA: *(handing a lunch pail to Addy)* Y'all be careful now. Go straight to school and come straight home after.

SARAH: *(hooking her arm in Addy's)* Don't worry, Mrs. Walker. I'm gonna look after Addy. I ain't gonna let nothing bad happen to her.

*(**Addy** and **Sarah** EXIT.)*

ACT TWO

Scene: The same morning, in the classroom. Addy and Sarah are seated together at a desk. Harriet sits at a desk in front of them.

*(**Miss Dunn** ENTERS. She stops next to Sarah.)*

MISS DUNN: Welcome back, Sarah. And who is your friend?

SARAH: This here is Addy Walker. She ain't never been to school before.

MISS DUNN: *(smiling in welcome)* I'm so pleased you're here, Addy. You may feel a bit confused this first week, but we'll help you learn your way.

ADDY: Thank you, ma'am.

*(**Miss Dunn** goes to the front of the classroom.)*

MISS DUNN: Good morning, boys and girls. I am Miss Dunn. I want you children who have been here before to help the new students. We'll begin our first day by copying the alphabet from the board. Sarah, please help Addy.

SARAH: Yes, ma'am. Look, Addy. *(demonstrating with the pencil)* Here's how you hold your pencil. And here's how you make the letters. *(She pushes the slate and pencil over to Addy.)* You try now.

*(**Addy** picks up the pencil, but it slips. She wraps her whole hand around it and struggles to make the letters as **Sarah** watches patiently and instructs her gently.)*

ADDY: My letters look squiggly and rough.

SARAH: *(encouraging)* Keep trying. *(She pauses as she watches Addy.)* Don't push down so hard. That's it. You doing fine.

(***Miss Dunn*** *approaches their desk and gently takes the slate pencil from Addy.)*

MISS DUNN: *(writes on Addy's slate)* This is your name, Addy. I want you to practice it.

(***Miss Dunn*** *gives the slate pencil back to Addy, then moves on toward the front of the room.)*

(***Addy*** *stares at the slate.* ***Sarah*** *nudges her.)*

SARAH: Addy, you're s'posed to practice writing that.

ADDY: I know. It's just…this the first time I ever saw my name wrote down.

(***Addy*** *writes her name, looks dissatisfied, erases it, and writes it again very slowly.* ***Sarah*** *looks at it.)*

SARAH: That's good, Addy. I can read that plain as day. *(spelling it out loud)* A-D-D-Y. You're good at learning.

ADDY: You're good at teaching.

(The two friends smile at each other.)

MISS DUNN: And now, boys and girls, I will assign permanent desk partners. Addy, you'll share a desk with Harriet.

SARAH: Miss Dunn, can Addy stay with me? I been helping her.

MISS DUNN: No, Sarah. I want Addy to sit near the front of the room.

(***Addy*** *stands up and walks to the front of the room. She smiles shyly as she sits next to Harriet.* ***Harriet*** *doesn't smile back.)*

HARRIET: Do you know the alphabet?

ADDY: I'm just learning it. Sarah was teaching me.

HARRIET: Sarah? Humph! *(in a snotty voice)* Sarah can hardly read herself! *I'll* help you. Miss Dunn put you with me because I'm the smartest one in the class.

ADDY: Sarah smart, too.

HARRIET: *(shakes her head in disagreement)* I'm named after Harriet Tubman. She helped run the Underground Railroad. You probably didn't know that. I know plenty of things like that. Now that Miss Dunn put you with me, I can teach you things. I might even invite you to study with me at my house.

ADDY: I bet your house is pretty.

HARRIET: Of course.

MISS DUNN: Boys and girls, it's time for lunch now.

*(**Harriet** rises quickly and EXITS with **Miss Dunn.**)*

*(**Sarah** gets out of her desk and crosses to Addy, who is still seated.)*

SARAH: How you like sitting with Harriet?

ADDY: She real smart and she got fine clothes. I wish I had a dress as pretty as the one she has on.

SARAH: Humph!

ADDY: What's the matter? Don't you like Harriet?

SARAH: That ain't it. Harriet don't like *me*. She all full of herself. She think she better than other people. If your family ain't got no money, she don't like you. And you know my family's poor.

ADDY: But Harriet was nice to me, and she know my family's poor.

SARAH: *(sincerely)* Listen, Addy. She was only nice 'cause Miss Dunn told her to be. Harriet don't have no poor girls like us for her friends. She gonna try to make you her slave. She tried it with me when I came to school last year, but I wouldn't let her. That's why she don't like me. She gonna hurt you just like she hurt me last year.

ADDY: *(hopefully)* Well, maybe Harriet changed from when you first come up here. Harriet ain't gonna hurt me. She say she got plenty to teach me, and I got plenty to learn.

*(**Harriet** ENTERS.)*

HARRIET: Addy, are you coming to lunch?

ADDY: Yes! Come on, Sarah.

SARAH: *(softly)* I ain't going with her.

HARRIET: *(in a snotty voice)* I heard you, Sarah. Nobody asked you to come. *(She turns away from Sarah.)* But you can come if you want, Addy. Sarah isn't the boss of you. It's your decision.

*(**Harriet** EXITS. **Addy** watches her go but does not follow her.)*

ACT THREE

Scene: Outside Mrs. Ford's dress shop, after school, about three weeks later.

*(**Sarah** and **Addy** ENTER, stage right, carrying lunch pails. **Sarah** carries a bunch of grapes, which the girls are sharing. The door to Mrs. Ford's dress shop is stage left. The girls talk and eat grapes as they walk slowly across the stage to the shop. They stop walking when they reach the door of the shop.)*

ADDY: *(worried)* Miss Dunn say we gonna have a spelling match in two weeks. I'm gonna have to spell better than I do now or I'll be put out in the first round of the match.

SARAH: But you only been in school three weeks now.

ADDY: But it seems like I ain't never gonna catch up. Younger girls can read and spell better than me. Maybe it's too late for me to learn.

SARAH: *(kindly)* It ain't never too late. You can't learn everything at once. Learning go slow. I didn't do so good on yesterday's spelling test, neither. I should've studied harder.

ADDY: *(frustrated)* I studied hard and I *still* didn't do good. *(stopping to face Sarah)* How many did you get right?

*(**Sarah** stops, too, and the girls face each other as they talk and share the grapes.)*

SARAH: How many did *you* get right?

ADDY: I asked first.

SARAH: Well, I got all twenty wrong 'cause I didn't study at all. *(sadly)* My poppa can't hardly find work, so my momma and me been taking in extra washing. Sometimes I ain't got time to do my lessons.

ADDY: I got twelve wrong. *(shaking her head)* You and me ain't like Harriet. You should see her papers. All 100s. She already doing multiplication. Schoolwork come easy to her. I bet she'll win the spelling match without hardly studying. And did you see that blue dress she had on yesterday? It was so pretty. I never even seen it before. She must have ten or fifteen dresses. *(She eats the last grape.)*

SARAH: *(annoyed)* Let's talk about something else. *(starting to walk again)* I don't like talking about Harriet, or even thinking about her.

ADDY: I do. Harriet has everything I dreamed freedom would bring me. She got fancy dresses. She smart. She sure of herself.

SARAH: *(sarcastically)* She sure is.

ADDY: Harriet say she gonna invite me to her house so we can study spelling together.

SARAH: *(matter-of-factly)* But she ain't invited you yet.

ADDY: No, not yet. I can't wait to see her house.

SARAH: *(firmly)* Addy, I done warned you about Harriet. She ain't...

*(**Sarah** is interrupted when **Momma** ENTERS, coming out of the door of the shop. She is carrying packages and crying.)*

ADDY: Momma, what's the matter?

MOMMA: *(wiping her eyes and blowing her nose)* I'm supposed to deliver these packages for Mrs. Ford. But I can't read the addresses, so I don't know where to go.

ADDY: *(taking the packages)* Sarah and I can deliver them, Momma. Sarah can read way better than me, and she know her way around Philadelphia.

SARAH: *(looking at the addresses on the packages)* I know where these streets is!

MOMMA: *(drying her eyes)* I guess I ain't got a right to this job because I ain't been honest about not reading. I gotta learn to read or find something else to do.

ADDY: *(touches Momma's arm)* Momma, I can teach you how to read. And I'll get practice from helping you.

MOMMA: I think it's too late for me to learn.

ADDY: *(enthusiastically)* Sarah say it ain't never too late.

SARAH: *(nods her head)* That's right!

MOMMA: *(hugs Sarah)* You a big help, Sarah. I don't know what we'd do without you.

ADDY: We'll have our first lesson tonight, Momma.

MOMMA: *(smiles and hugs Addy)* All right, Addy. I'll try. Ain't no change coming overnight, but by and by maybe we'll both learn.

ADDY: We will, Momma. You'll see!

*(**Addy** and **Sarah** EXIT with the packages.)*

ACT FOUR

Scene: Outside Mrs. Ford's dress shop, after school, two weeks later.

*(**Addy** and **Sarah** ENTER, carrying lunch pails and books. They stop when **Addy** bends down to tie her boot lace.)*

SARAH: You ready for the spelling match tomorrow?

ADDY: I hope so. I been studying every night.

*(**Harriet** and **Mavis** ENTER, carrying books and lunch pails. **Addy** picks up her lunch pail and books and stands up again.)*

HARRIET: *(ignoring Sarah)* Well, Addy, are you going to walk home with Mavis and me today, or do you have to ask Sarah's permission?

ADDY: I don't have to ask her permission. *(excitedly)* I'm gonna walk with you.

HARRIET: *(smugly)* Good.

ADDY: *(turns to smile at Sarah)* Sarah, you can come, too.

SARAH: No, I can't. You go on. You know you want to. *(She blinks hard to fight back tears.)* I don't care.

*(**Sarah** turns away and EXITS.)*

*(**Addy** watches Sarah leave. **Harriet** and **Mavis** pile their books on top of Addy's.)*

ADDY: These are kinda heavy. Why I got to carry them all?

HARRIET: *(firmly)* You're the new girl. You have to do what we say.

MAVIS: That's right.

(***Harriet*** *and* ***Mavis*** *look at each other and giggle. Then, as they all begin to walk along,* ***Harriet*** *takes an apple out of her pocket or her lunch pail.)*

HARRIET: Did you see Sarah's dress today? It was so wrinkled, it looked like she slept in it. *(She throws the apple in the air once or twice, then tosses it to Mavis.)*

MAVIS: *(dropping behind Addy to catch the apple)* And it had a big brown stain on the front.

ADDY: *(struggling not to drop all the books as she watches them toss the apple)* That don't matter.

HARRIET: *(catching the apple again)* Of course it matters. Anyway, what do you care about Sarah? You're on our side now. At least *you* look presentable.

(By this time the girls are in front of the door to Mrs. Ford's dress shop, where they stop. ***Harriet*** *and* ***Mavis*** *exchange a look. They take their books back.* ***Harriet*** *takes a bite of the apple.)*

MAVIS: This is where you live, isn't it, Addy?

ADDY: Yes, but I thought I was going home with y'all today. Momma said I can study at your house, Harriet.

HARRIET: I don't think so. Not today.

ADDY: *(protesting)* But the spelling match is tomorrow. You promised...

HARRIET: *(firmly)* Not today. Come on, Mavis.

(***Harriet*** *and* ***Mavis*** EXIT, *hurrying away. Addy is left alone, looking very sad.)*

ACT FIVE

Scene: In the classroom, the next morning. Addy, Harriet, and Sarah stand in a line facing Miss Dunn for the spelling match.

MISS DUNN: Harriet, spell "carriage."

HARRIET: *(spelling quickly)* C-A-R-R-I-A-G-E.

MISS DUNN: Sarah, you have the next word. Spell "button."

SARAH: *(slowly and carefully)* B-U-T-T-O-N.

MISS DUNN: Addy, it's your turn. Spell "tomorrow."

ADDY: T-O-M-O-R-O *(She stops and starts again.)* T-O-M-O-R-R-O-W.

MISS DUNN: Correct.

HARRIET: *(whispers to Addy)* I'm going to win, and my mother said I can have friends over after school for ice cream to celebrate. I might ask you.

*(**Addy** smiles.)*

*(**Sarah** looks at Addy and Harriet and turns away unhappily.)*

MISS DUNN: Harriet, spell "doctor."

HARRIET: *(quickly)* D-O-C-T-O-R.

MISS DUNN: Sarah, spell "account."

SARAH: A-C-C- *(She stops and starts again, unsure.)* A-C-C-O-N-T.

MISS DUNN: I'm sorry. That's not correct.

*(**Sarah** sits down, looking disappointed.)*

HARRIET: *(whispers to Addy)* I can't believe Sarah missed such an easy one. She is so dumb.

MISS DUNN: Addy, now you must spell "account."

ADDY: A-C-C-O-U-N-T.

MISS DUNN: Good, Addy. Harriet, only you and Addy are left. Spell "principle." We all live our lives by *principles.* "Principle."

HARRIET: P-R-I-N-S-I-P-L-E.

MISS DUNN: I'm sorry. That is not correct. Addy, you must spell the word correctly to win. "Principle."

ADDY: P-R-I-N-C-I-P-L-E.

MISS DUNN: *(delightedly)* Correct! Addy Walker, you have truly earned this prize. Your hard work has paid off.

*(**Miss Dunn** pins a medal on Addy, who beams with pride.)*

MISS DUNN: Congratulations, Addy. And now, you are all excused for lunch. *(She turns to erase the chalkboard.)*

HARRIET: *(smugly)* Well, if I had studied at all, I would have beaten you. Anyway, Miss Dunn gave you easier words. *(She crosses to the door and looks back at Addy.)* I'm eating lunch out on the front steps if you want to join me and my friends.

*(Hearing what Harriet has said, **Sarah** puts her head down on her desk.)*

*(**Harriet** EXITS, flouncing out.)*

MISS DUNN: *(crosses to Addy and puts her hands on Addy's shoulders)* This is a very special day for you, Addy. But you don't look very happy.

ADDY: *(sadly)* Miss Dunn, I done hurt Sarah, and I wouldn't blame her if she never spoke to me again.

MISS DUNN: *(looks over at Sarah, whose head is still down)* But I am sure she would *listen* to you. Why don't you go talk to her and tell her how you feel?

*(**Miss Dunn** EXITS.)*

*(**Addy** thinks for a few seconds, then goes to her desk to look inside her lunch pail. She carries it back to Sarah's desk.)*

ADDY: *(sitting next to Sarah, who looks up)* I'm so sorry, Sarah. Please forgive me. I wanted to be friends with Harriet because she's popular and smart and rich. But she ain't a real friend. *(pauses)* I know you is. I never meant to hurt you. *(holds out her hand)* I want you to still be my friend.

SARAH: *(taking Addy's hand)* I still want to be your friend. *(pauses, then smiles)* And I wanted you to win the spelling match so bad.

ADDY: I wanted you to win, too. I was sad when you missed your word. Maybe we can study spelling together right now. *(She reaches into her lunch pail and smiles as she pulls something out of it. She holds out four cookies on her outstretched hand, each in the shape of a letter.)* Look, Sarah. Momma made me cookies in the shapes of the letters I'm teaching her. Here's our first word!

*(As **Addy** hands the cookies one at a time to Sarah, they spell the letters out loud together.)*

ADDY and **SARAH:** L-O-V-E.

ADDY: *(smiling)* Love's the best word to start with.

Friendship and Freedom

A Play About Addy

Putting on the Play

Contents

Play Summary

The play takes place in the fall of 1864. Nine-year-old Addy Walker and her mother have escaped from slavery and settled in Philadelphia. As the play begins, Addy is about to start school for the first time. So far, freedom has not been what she expected. She and her mother live in a dark, dreary *garret*, or attic. Her mother works long hours as a seamstress and Addy hardly ever gets to see her. Worst of all, they still don't know where Addy's father and brother are. Going to school for the first time is exciting, because Addy will be able to learn to read. But Addy learns more in school than just reading and writing. She learns about friendship and freedom as well.

ADDY ✺ 1864

Addy's story is one shared by many African Americans who lived during Addy's time. The courage they needed to survive and escape from slavery helped them face the choices and challenges of freedom.

THE CHARACTERS

HOW TO BECOME YOUR CHARACTER

❋ *Close your eyes and imagine that you are your character. Then practice walking, talking, and moving as you think your character would.*

❋ *Your imagination is your best tool for a successful performance. If you don't have a stage or elaborate costumes or props, act as if you do!*

ADDY

SARAH

MOMMA

To prepare for your role, study your character description. Check the script to see what other characters say about or to your character. Use those statements as clues to how you should act.

Addy is nine years old. She is bright, loving, and hopeful. She has faced the many changes in her life with courage. Now she must find the courage to deal with the choices and challenges that freedom brings.

Sarah is a nine-year-old girl who is Addy's best friend. She has a wide, warm smile and a face that shows her feelings. She believes in speaking her mind, and she is a loyal friend.

Momma is Addy's mother. She works hard as a seamstress and hopes that her family will be reunited soon in Philadelphia. She is a strong, calm woman who can comfort her daughter with a hug and a word.

Miss Dunn is Addy's teacher. She is warm and kind to her students, but when she has something important to say, her firm voice rings out strongly through the classroom.

MISS DUNN

Harriet is a rich, snobby nine-year-old classmate of Addy's. She speaks loudly and flounces when she walks to draw attention to herself and to show what she thinks of everyone else.

HARRIET

MAVIS

Mavis is Harriet's friend and is also nine years old. Like Harriet, she is mean to the other girls.

Four people can perform *Friendship and Freedom* if one actor takes the parts of Momma and Harriet and another actor takes the parts of Miss Dunn and Mavis. "Extras" can play other students in the classroom scenes or passersby in the outside scenes.

IF YOU FORGET YOUR LINES . . .

❋ *If you forget your lines and can't hear the prompter, just think about what your character would say and then* ***ad-lib*** *(say it in your own words).*

THE DIRECTOR

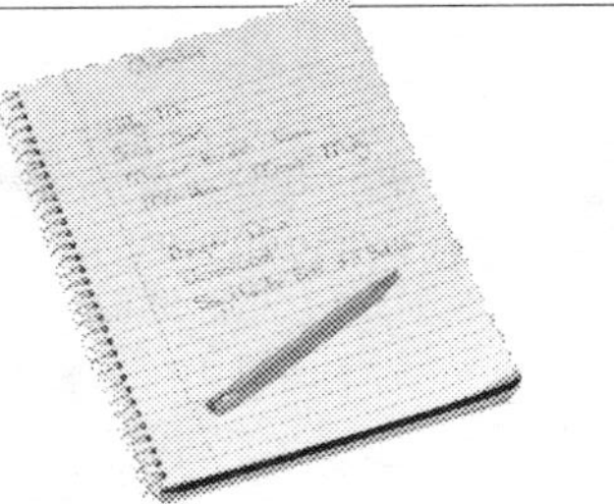

PRAISING THE ACTORS

✹ *One of your most important jobs as director is to praise the actors. Watch for good things that happen during rehearsals and make them part of the finished performance. The best praise is specific and sincere. Keep a notebook handy for your notes about things to remember and praise.*

One of the director's jobs is to help an actor "get into character" by helping him or her imagine what it would be like to truly be that character. How would a character show joy or anger? For example, would one character show joy by laughing aloud while another smiled quietly? Would a character stamp her foot in anger or turn her back?

Encourage actors to practice walking and talking as their characters. How would the main character of the play walk? How would her voice change when she is happy or upset? Helping the actors find answers to these kinds of questions will create a more believable performance.

BLOCKING THE ACTION

As the director, you help the actors plan how to move when they are onstage. This is called *blocking the action,* and it usually takes place during rehearsal. The script sometimes tells the actors how and when to move, but it is your job to give additional directions. You also give the actors little signs, or *cues,* about when to go onstage and offstage.

When you are blocking the action, try to use the whole stage. Important action should take place near the front of the stage, close to the audience.

Actors should face the audience most of the time when they're speaking, so the audience can see the actors' faces and hear their lines. But sometimes you might ask an actor to turn away to show sadness or rejection.

KEEPING THE PLAY MOVING

Keep the play moving by helping the actors *overlap* their lines. To overlap, an actor says her first word just as the actor before says her last word. Combine overlapping with occasional pauses to make the play more lively and natural.

DIRECTOR'S TIPS

✹ *Make sure that all actors speak clearly and loudly enough to be heard.*

✹ *Help the actors "get into character" by asking questions about what their characters are like.*

✹ *Remind the actors to relax as they say their lines. Using props will help them move naturally.*

✹ *Plan the action so that the audience can see the actors' faces.*

✹ *Remind the actors not to stand between other actors and the audience.*

The Crew

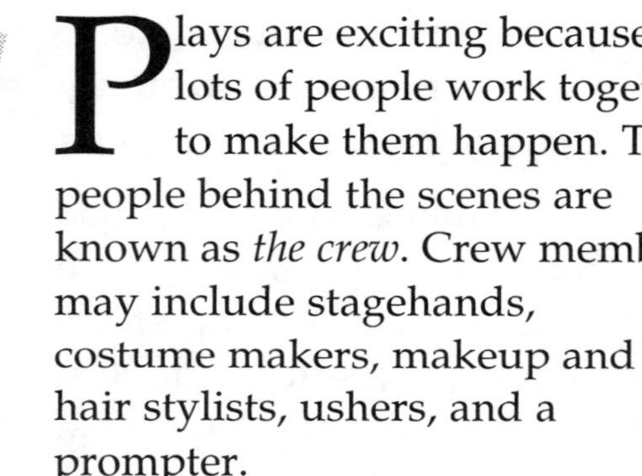

Music and Mood

✹ *Before the show and during set changes and intermissions, set the mood with music. Songs of the Civil War era or spirituals such as "This Little Light of Mine" or "Swing Low, Sweet Chariot" will create the mood of Addy's world in 1864. Your librarian should be able to help you find the right music.*

Just before the play starts, the stagehand in charge of music can ***fade out*** *the music by gradually lowering the volume until it can no longer be heard.*

Plays are exciting because lots of people work together to make them happen. The people behind the scenes are known as *the crew*. Crew members may include stagehands, costume makers, makeup and hair stylists, ushers, and a prompter.

Stagehands create sets by finding, building, and painting scenery. They also change the scenery between acts and operate the curtain.

The *sound crew* creates sound effects and operates the sound system.

The *lights crew* operates the lighting system.

The *stage manager* works closely with the director to manage what happens onstage. He or she marks the script with every sound or light cue and all set changes, and then makes sure every cue comes on time.

The *property master* or *property mistress* is responsible for finding or making *properties*—or *props*—and for having the props ready at the right time and in the right place. That way, the actors have exactly what they need each time they go onstage.

Costume makers help the actors find or make costumes. *Makeup* and *hair stylists* help the actors put on makeup and style their hair or wigs.

The *prompter* follows the play line by line in a script book and whispers lines from offstage if an actor forgets them.

Ushers take tickets and lead the audience to their seats. They are sometimes in charge of getting playbills, programs, and tickets ready for the show.

At the end of the performance, everyone who helped put on the show should take a bow at the curtain call!

THE COSTUMES

COSTUME TIPS

✹ *The very simplest way to identify characters doesn't even require costumes! An actor can wear a sign around his or her neck with the character's name printed large enough for the audience to read. This way, actors can easily switch parts without having to switch costumes!*

✹ *A long-sleeved white shirt with the sleeves tied around the waist makes a fine half-apron for Momma.*

Costumes help bring a play to life and identify characters—but you can have a great performance without costumes, too!

Addy wears a white long-sleeved blouse with a bow and a calf-length skirt and matching jacket. She wears dark stockings and black ankle boots. Her hair is tied back with a ribbon. She wears small hoop earrings.

Sarah wears a plain long-sleeved, calf-length dress, dark stockings, and dark ankle boots. Her hair is cut short and she wears small earrings.

Momma wears a simple long-sleeved, ankle-length dress, dark stockings, and ankle boots. Her hair is pulled back into a low bun and she wears earrings. She may also wear an apron and hang a tape measure around her neck.

Miss Dunn's clothes are the same style as Momma's, but they are nicer. She may wear a shawl. Her hair is pulled back into a low bun and held in place with a *snood*, or small net. She wears earrings and may wear glasses.

Harriet wears a fancy long-sleeved, calf-length dress with a full skirt, dark stockings, and dark ankle boots. Her hair is long and loose, and she wears a puffy bow that matches her dress. She also wears earrings.

Mavis's clothes are the same style as Harriet's, but a little less fancy. She wears a simple hair ribbon and earrings.

QUICK CHANGES

✹ *Practice making quick costume changes. An actor who plays both Momma and Harriet can remove Momma's apron and tape measure at the end of Act One and add a full petticoat under her skirt to play Harriet. She can also let her hair go loose and add a fancy hair bow.*

✹ *An actor playing Miss Dunn and Mavis will change costumes twice. The actor should remove Miss Dunn's glasses and shawl and exchange the snood for a hair ribbon to play Mavis.*

✹ *Quick changes will be easier if costumes and props are always left in the same place backstage.*

STAGE SETS

SCENES

ACT ONE
Early morning in the garret where Addy and Momma live

ACT TWO
At school

ACT THREE
Outside Mrs. Ford's dress shop, after school

ACT FOUR
Outside Mrs. Ford's dress shop, after school

ACT FIVE
At school

Friendship and Freedom has three indoor scenes and two outdoor scenes. You will need three sets. You can use the same basic set, but change the way it looks between acts.

One way to create a background is by using large paper to make a mural. Light-brown paper across the back of your stage works best. You can make cutouts to pin or lightly tape to the mural so you can change them from scene to scene. Use paint or chalk to add details to the cutouts and mural. Applying paint with a large sponge is fast and adds texture.

A simple table, two chairs, and a folding cot can set the scene in the garret.

Push pairs of chairs together in rows to make the double desks in the classroom. Put a chair and small table at the front for the teacher. Paint a large rectangle of paper or poster board black to

look like a blackboard and hang it on your background or at the front of the room. Put books and a globe on a table or the teacher's desk.

The door of the dress shop could be a real opening cut into the background. Or it could be painted on one edge of the background, so that the actors can come around the side of the background as if they were coming through a door.

LIGHTING

Use lights to set the mood. It is a little dark inside the garret in Act One. The classroom in Acts Two and Five should be brighter. Acts Three and Four take place outside in bright afternoon light.

In the garret.

At school.

Outside Mrs. Ford's dress shop.

PROPS

PROPS

ACT ONE
Two lunch pails
Hair ribbons

ACT TWO
A slate
A slate pencil

ACT THREE
Two lunch pails
A bunch of grapes
Schoolbooks
Packages of clothes
A handkerchief

ACT FOUR
Four lunch pails
Schoolbooks
An apple

ACT FIVE
A medal
A lunch pail
L-O-V-E cookies

Here are some ideas for making or finding the props in this play.

For the lunch pails use small tin or plastic pails, or baskets with handles. You can easily cover the plastic pails or baskets with tinfoil to make them look like metal. Tie a scrap of brightly colored fabric to each handle. Scraps like this helped children identify their lunch pails.

The slates can be small chalk-boards. You can use pieces of chalk for the slate pencils. To make the packages of clothes, wrap clothing, old sheets, or crumpled newspaper in brown paper and tie string around them. Use a marker to write a name and address on each package.

The medal could be a pretty pin borrowed from someone. Or you could make a medal like those described on page 14. The cookies can be cut out of tan construction paper or cardboard.

THE STAGE

There are special terms to describe the front, back, and sides of the stage. These terms were used by actors and directors long ago, and are still used today.

Stages used to be built on a slant, with the back part of the stage higher than the front. This angle allowed the audience to see the actors better. The terms *upstage* and *downstage* come from the way the stage slanted. *Upstage* is the area farthest from the audience—the area that used to be higher. *Downstage* is the front of the stage, nearest the audience. An actor standing in the exact middle of the stage is at *center stage.*

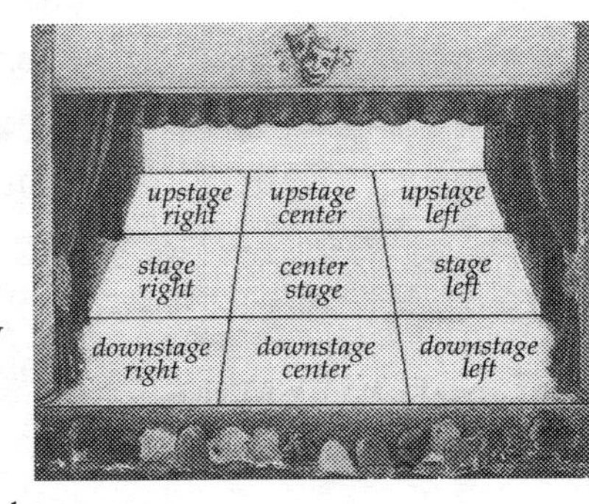

When an actor stands at center stage, facing the audience, the area to the actor's right is *stage right* and the area to the actor's left is *stage left*. The best way to remember *stage right* and *stage left* is to face the audience.

MAKING A MEDAL

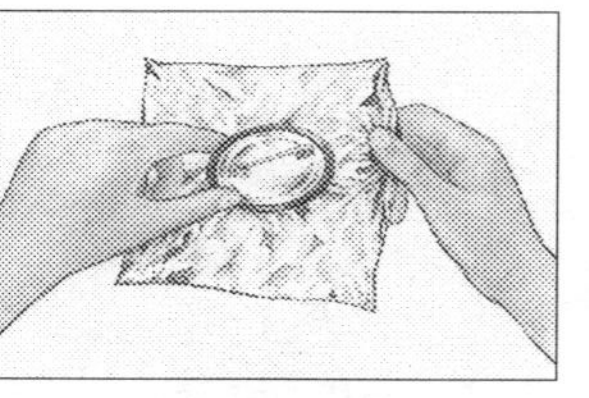

PIN-ON BUTTON
Be careful not to poke yourself as you wrap the button!

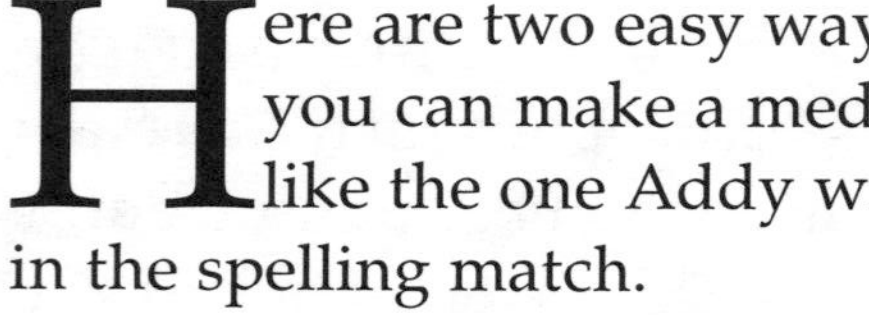

Here are two easy ways you can make a medal like the one Addy wins in the spelling match.

USING A PIN-ON BUTTON

First, find a pin-on button—the kind that has a slogan or funny saying—that is about 1 to 1½ inches in diameter. Cover the button with tinfoil so that the face of the medal is smooth and shiny. To make the medal look fancier, tape or glue a piece of blue or red ribbon to the bottom of the button. Use a ribbon that's a different color from Addy's outfit. The ribbon should be about the same width as the button. Trim the bottom of the ribbon into a "V" shape, as shown. The button can be pinned on Addy's jacket by Miss Dunn in the last act of the play.

USING A REGULAR BUTTON

Begin with a regular button that is 1 to 1½ inches wide. Cover it with tinfoil so that the front is smooth and shiny. Then cut a small piece of poster board or lightweight cardboard about 2 inches across and ½ inch high. Cut the corners so that they are slightly rounded. Cover the poster board with a small piece of tinfoil and make it a little wrinkled to give it texture. Then attach the button to the foil strip with a piece of clear tape across the back of the button and the strip. You can color the wrinkled tinfoil with a yellow marker to make it look gold.

Put a small loop of masking tape or adhesive tape on the back of the poster board piece so that Miss Dunn can attach the medal to Addy's jacket. Or use Scotch tape to attach a safety pin to the back of the "medal."

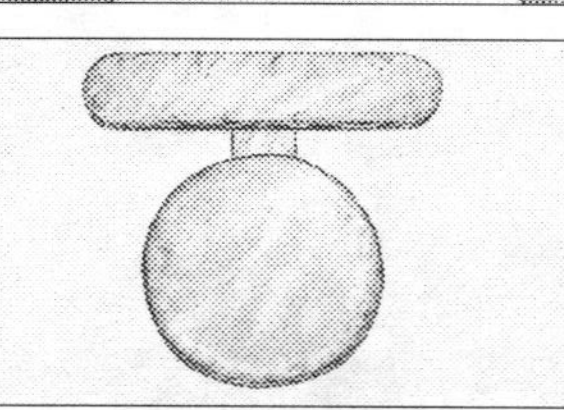

REGULAR BUTTON
Use a small loop of tape to attach this medal to Addy's jacket.

TEA FOR FELICITY

A play in five acts about Felicity Merriman, a nine-year-old girl living in Williamsburg, Virginia, in 1774. It is just before the American Revolution, and many colonists want independence from England. The play opens as Felicity—who is struggling for her own independence—starts lessons in becoming a young lady.

ADMIT ONE
TEA FOR FELICITY
Date ______________ Time ______________
Place ______________
Admit One
Seat ____

HOME IS WHERE THE HEART IS

A play in five acts about Kirsten Larson, a nine-year-old Swedish immigrant who comes to America in 1854. The play begins as Kirsten and her family arrive in New York. Now they must start another long journey to their new home on the Minnesota frontier.

ADMIT ONE
HOME IS WHERE THE HEART IS
Date ______________ Time ______________
Place ______________
Admit One
Seat ____

FRIENDSHIP AND FREEDOM

A play in five acts about Addy Walker, a nine-year-old girl who escapes from slavery during the Civil War and makes a new life for herself in freedom. The play starts as Addy gets ready for her first day of school in Philadelphia.

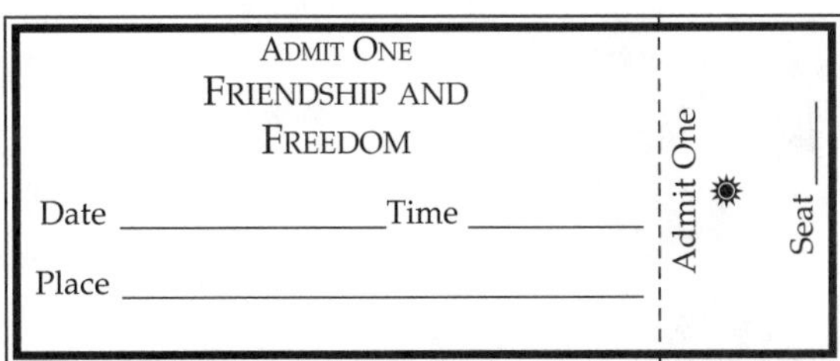
ADMIT ONE
FRIENDSHIP AND FREEDOM
Date ______________ Time ______________
Place ______________
Admit One
Seat ____

ACTIONS SPEAK LOUDER THAN WORDS

A play in five acts about Samantha Parkington, a nine-year-old orphan living with her wealthy grandmother and learning to be a proper young lady. The play takes place in the summer of 1904, in a small town near New York City.

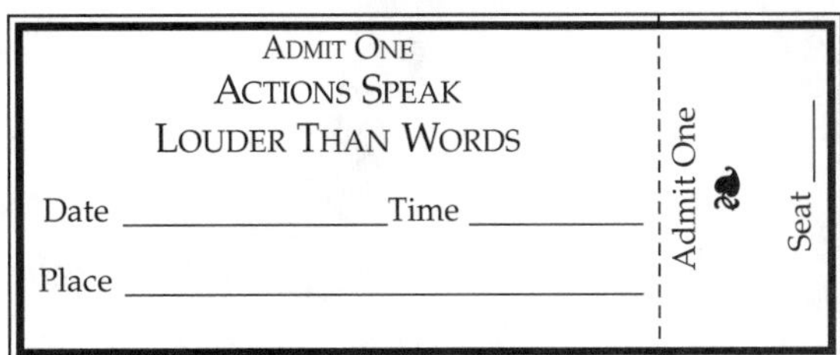
ADMIT ONE
ACTIONS SPEAK LOUDER THAN WORDS
Date ______________ Time ______________
Place ______________
Admit One
Seat ____

WAR ON THE HOME FRONT

A play in three acts about nine-year-old Molly McIntire and her dreams of a perfect Halloween during World War Two. The play starts as Molly and her friends Linda and Susan plan their costumes in Molly's backyard.

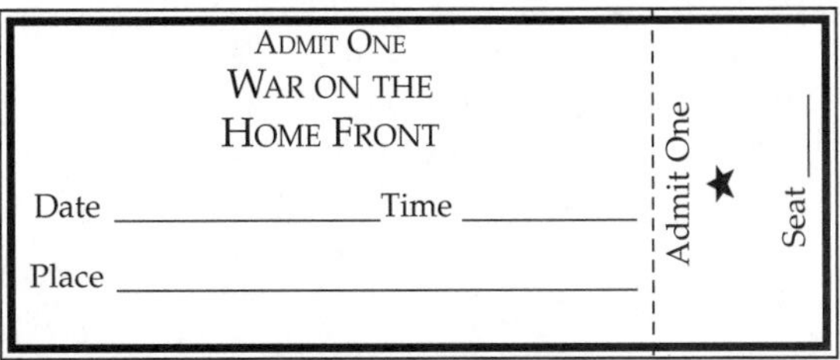
ADMIT ONE
WAR ON THE HOME FRONT
Date ______________ Time ______________
Place ______________
Admit One
Seat ____

You may use these play titles and descriptions with the program blackline master on page 65 to create play programs. For tickets, photocopy or make tickets like these.

Actions Speak Louder Than Words

America's New Century—1904

Samantha ❧ 1904

Samantha lived at a time when America was changing rapidly. Factories produced new and inexpensive goods for many Americans—especially wealthy people like Grandmary—but life was hard for those who worked in the factories.

About the Play

Actions Speak Louder Than Words is a play about nine-year-old Samantha Parkington, an orphan living with her wealthy grandmother in 1904.

At the turn of the century, America was popping with newfangled notions and amazing inventions. New machines in factories produced toys, clothing, and furniture for wealthy Americans like Samantha and her grandmother. Cities like New York were crowded with people who worked in factories to produce these goods. Young children from poor families sometimes had to work in factories to earn money for their families, so they could not go to school.

Actions Speak Louder Than Words takes place in the summer of 1904, in a small town near New York City, where Samantha lives with Grandmary. Samantha is hard at work trying earn a beautiful doll by working diligently on her sampler and by behaving well. Grandmary expects Samantha to always behave like a proper young lady, but Samantha sometimes has a hard time accepting all the rules about what a young lady may and may not do.

Samantha has been lonely living with Grandmary. She longs for the doll so she'll have someone to play with. But then Nellie comes to work as a servant at the Rylands' house next door, and Samantha and Nellie quickly become best friends. Samantha is shocked to learn that Nellie has left her family in the city to come to work at the Rylands'. But Nellie says being a servant is better than the factory job she had in the city, where the industrial dust hurt her lungs and made her cough. Samantha is also shocked to learn that Nellie has never gone to school.

When Nellie is made to leave the Rylands' because she cannot stop coughing, Samantha is disconsolate. She does the only thing she can do: she gives Nellie her most precious possession to take back to the city.

Samantha's delight at finding a new friend is tempered by her concern for Nellie's well-being. Reading and dramatizing *Actions Speak Louder Than Words* will help your students understand what it was like to live in a rapidly changing world that offered much to delight—but sometimes at the expense of children. The related activity will help your students think about what types of behavior are considered proper and appropriate for girls and boys—in Samantha's time and today. This firsthand experience will help them approach the play with more understanding, both as performers and as members of the audience.

Historical Context

At the turn of the twentieth century, America was becoming increasingly industrialized. Inventions such as the telephone, the automobile, and electric lights were changing people's lives profoundly and quickly. Factories were producing new and inexpensive goods for many Americans, but life for the factory workers was often hard and dangerous.

Grandmary's comfortable and proper world was made possible because of servants. The servants' long hours of hard work behind the scenes made life comfortable for Samantha and Grandmary and allowed them to live in their elegant, elaborate, and large home.

Even though the life of a servant was hard, there were many people eager to do the work. Large numbers of immigrants arrived in America every year, many of them very poor. Immigration peaked in 1907, when more immigrants than ever before arrived in America. They were willing to take any work to help their families survive. Immigrants—especially those who didn't speak English—usually had little choice of jobs other than as servants or factory workers.

Life was especially hard on the many children who worked in factories. Long hours, inadequate ventilation, and unsafe conditions created serious health hazards.

CHILD LABOR

Many children from poor families had to work in factories or as servants instead of going to school. While wealthy children like Samantha and Eddie went to school and were taught to become proper young ladies and gentlemen, hundreds of thousands of poor children—like Nellie—worked hard every day.

Child labor was almost entirely unregulated until the early 1900s. In 1903, Illinois was the first state to limit the workday of children under 16 to eight hours. The first federal regulation of child labor finally passed in 1916.

Working ten and twelve hours a day left only a few hours in the evening for schooling. By then, most children were too exhausted to stay awake, so many factory children received little or no education. It wasn't until 1916 that federal child labor laws finally limited the number of hours per day that children could work.

Themes in the Play

Actions Speak Louder Than Words could be included in social studies units about life at the turn of the century or the Industrial Revolution. It could also be used in thematic units dealing with child labor, friendship, education, families, or change.

Preparing to Perform—Etiquette

> Etiquette
>
> ***Objectives:***
> *To write etiquette guides for young men and women*
>
> *To compare and contrast etiquette today with that of the past*
>
> *To consider stereotypes and gender socialization*
>
> ***Teacher's Role:*** *Facilitator*
>
> ***Student Roles:*** *First as writers of "Guides to Etiquette," then in role in frozen images*
>
> ***Time Needed:*** *40 minutes*
>
> ***Space Needed:*** *An open space*
>
> ***Materials Needed:*** *Paper, pens, and pencils*

Through her friendship with Nellie, Samantha learns about the life of the working poor. But in Samantha's privileged world, her entire upbringing and education are focused on teaching her to be a proper young lady. This activity will help your students think about what being "proper" meant for boys and girls in Samantha's time. It will help them think about what is considered "proper" for boys and girls today, and consider how rules of behavior have or have not changed over the past 90 years.

Context

Grandmary hopes to mold Samantha into a proper young lady. Grandmary's neighbor, Mrs. Ryland, wants her son Eddie to behave properly as well. Your students can discover exactly what this meant in Samantha's time, and can decide if there is a modern-day equivalent.

Directions

1. Writing assignment: Divide the class into four groups—either mixed-gender groups or two groups of girls and two of boys. Each group will write an etiquette guide for boys or girls in 1904 or today. You can decide which group writes which guide, or let the students decide. The guides should include five to ten rules about behavior. The guides need not all have the same categories, but some overlap would be interesting. To help the students get started, the whole class could brainstorm possible categories and make a list on the chalkboard before breaking into groups. Categories might include instruction on the proper way to talk to adults, how to interact with the opposite sex, how to dress for school, how to behave at meals, or how to entertain yourself on a rainy afternoon. Categories could be gender-specific and period-specific, such as how to sit or walk, or how to dress for an afternoon tea. Once the students are in their groups, allow at least 15 minutes for brainstorming and writing. After they finish writing, they should plan a tableau or a brief pantomime that demonstrates one of the points of etiquette.

2. Sharing and dramatizing the guides: Ask each group to share its etiquette guide by first reading the instructions aloud and then presenting its tableau or pantomime—but without telling the class which point of etiquette is being demonstrated. The rest of the class will analyze the image and guess which point of etiquette is being dramatized. For example, the 1904 *Guide to Etiquette for Young Ladies* might have a rule that young ladies should speak only when spoken to, and then answer politely. Two students might come forward and sit silently for a moment. One would ask the other a question; the second student would respond politely and respectfully.

This part of the activity may be especially challenging if students have to represent the opposite gender. But the very act of dramatizing rules for boys or girls allows students to compare different expectations of the behavior of boys and of girls, both in the past and today.

After each group has presented its guide and its tableau or pantomime, ask if another group would like to try dramatizing the same idea in another way.

3. Discussion: Students may return to their desks or remain in their small groups for the discussion. What were and are the differences between expectations for girls and boys? Do those differences make sense? What are the differences between 1904 and today? What has stayed the same? Why might some things have stayed the same? How did it feel to represent someone of the opposite gender? What is a gender stereotype? Did you see any today in your performances? What is gender socialization? Why might it exist?

Consider having books of etiquette available in your classroom for students to use for research for this project. Students could also interview older people about manners and etiquette.

THEATER AT THE TURN OF THE CENTURY

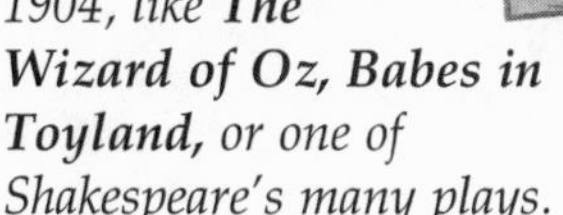

In 1904, Samantha and Grandmary might have spent a day in New York City and gone to a matinee performance of one of the plays that were popular in 1904, like ***The Wizard of Oz, Babes in Toyland,*** *or one of Shakespeare's many plays.*

The Wizard of Oz *was first performed in 1903.*

TABLEAUX VIVANTS

Students can create ***tableaux vivants*** *(ta-BLOW vee-VAHN), or* ***living pictures*** *(also referred to as* ***frozen images****), to dramatize critical ideas in this activity.*

Creating ***tableaux vivants*** *was a popular parlor game at the turn of the century, when Samantha was a girl. People posed as famous paintings or important events in history while others guessed the painting or scene. This scene was called "Farewell to the Mayflower."*

Actions Speak Louder Than Words

A Play About Samantha

Play Script

TIPS FOR ACTORS

❧ Use your imagination. If you don't have a fancy stage or elaborate props and costumes, act as if you do!

❧ Speak clearly and loudly enough to be heard. Don't turn your back to the audience or stand between another actor and the audience.

❧ Pretend that you **are** the character you are playing. If you forget your lines and can't hear the prompter, think about what the character would really say and say it in your own words.

❧ Act and speak at the same time. Directions before your lines will tell you things to do as you are saying those lines. For example,

*(**Samantha** and **Nellie** roll their eyes, shake their heads, and groan.)*

NELLIE: That Eddie!

❧ Other directions make suggestions about how to say a line. For example,

SAMANTHA: *(almost crying)* What will I do without you, Nellie?

❧ Cooperate with the director and the other actors. And don't forget to smile at the curtain call!

Actions Speak Louder Than Words

A Play About Samantha

Characters

SAMANTHA
A nine-year-old orphan who lives with her wealthy grandmother

NELLIE
Samantha's best friend, who is also nine years old and who lives—and works—next door

GRANDMARY
Samantha's old-fashioned grandmother, who is trying to teach her proper values

UNCLE GARD
Samantha's favorite uncle, who calls her Sam

EDDIE RYLAND
Samantha's bratty neighbor, who loves to pester her

MRS. RYLAND
Eddie's snobby mother, who has hired Nellie as a maid

The action takes place in the summer of 1904, in and around Grandmary's house in a small town near New York City.

1

ACT ONE

Scene: Grandmary's very proper parlor. Uncle Gard and Grandmary are having tea.

*(**Samantha** ENTERS. She curtsies as she greets Grandmary, then hugs Uncle Gard.)*

SAMANTHA: Good afternoon, Grandmary. Uncle Gard! Hello!

UNCLE GARD: Hello, Sam! How would my best girl like to go for a drive?

SAMANTHA: In your automobile? I'd love to! Oh, Grandmary, may I?

GRANDMARY: *(gently)* No, my dear, not until after tea. Now come sit down and work on your sampler.

SAMANTHA: Yes, Grandmary.

*(**Samantha** sits down near Uncle Gard and picks up her sampler. **Uncle Gard** leans over to look at it.)*

UNCLE GARD: By Jupiter, Sam! What a fine sampler! What does it say?

SAMANTHA: *(proudly)* It's going to say "Actions speak louder than words." But I'm not quite finished yet.

UNCLE GARD: *(teasing)* Well, I bet actions take longer than words, too. *(smiling)* It looks like you've been stitching for a long time.

SAMANTHA: Yes, I've been working and working on it, Uncle Gard. And I'm practicing the piano for an hour every day, and trying to keep my clothes tidy, and trying not to get in any scrapes with Eddie Ryland, too. Because I'm earning a doll.

UNCLE GARD: Earning a doll?

SAMANTHA: *(excitedly)* Yes, the most beautiful doll in the world. You should see her, Uncle Gard! *(shows Uncle Gard a photo of her mother)* She looks just like my mother did, so I have named her Lydia. Grandmary said I can earn her by acting like a proper young lady.

GRANDMARY: That's right. I said we shall see how well you do.

UNCLE GARD: You must want that doll very much, Sam.

SAMANTHA: Oh yes, Uncle Gard. I do! She would be my best friend. The only person I can play with now is Eddie Ryland. *(making a face)* And he's not a friend, he's a pest!

GRANDMARY: Samantha! Young ladies do not call people pests.

SAMANTHA: *(apologizing)* I'm sorry, Grandmary. It's awfully hard to act like a lady when I think about Eddie. He's always teasing. The other day he said a girl was coming to live at his house. He probably made that up! *(sincerely)* But I wish it were true. I'd like having a girl next door to be my friend.

UNCLE GARD: I can see why you need that doll, Sam. Maybe I'd better help you earn it. Shall I try to do some stitches for you? Now let's see. Where's the top of this thing?

*(**Uncle Gard** takes the sampler and twists it all around, looking confused.)*

SAMANTHA: *(laughs)* No, thank you, Uncle Gard. That wouldn't be fair. I'd better do it myself!

GRANDMARY: *(smiling)* You've done quite well, Samantha. I've been very pleased with your efforts these past weeks. You've shown me by your actions that you can be a young lady. I think you have earned this.

*(**Grandmary** hands Samantha a fancy box. **Samantha** opens it and finds a doll.)*

SAMANTHA: Oh! Oh, Grandmary! Oh, she's even more beautiful than I remembered! Thank you! I love her!

GRANDMARY: *(tenderly)* Take good care of her, my dear.

SAMANTHA: I will! She'll be my finest treasure. I'll keep her forever and ever. I promise I will.

*(**Samantha** hugs the doll happily.)*

ACT TWO

Scene: The lilac hedge between Grandmary's house and the Rylands' house. Samantha is sitting on a garden bench playing with her doll.

*(**Eddie** ENTERS.)*

EDDIE: BOO!

SAMANTHA: Go away, Eddie.

EDDIE: *(teasing)* Nah, nah, Samantha, you're so dumb, you—Hey! What's that? *(pointing at Lydia)*

SAMANTHA: It's a doll.

EDDIE: *(making a face)* It's dumb.

SAMANTHA: Eddie, if you don't get out of here right now, I will take your entire beetle collection from behind the shed and put it in the offering plate at church on Sunday. *(holds doll tightly)* And I'll tell your mother you did it.

EDDIE: *(moves away)* Okay, I'll go. *(turns back, pouting)* I was going to tell you about Nellie, the new girl at our house, but now I won't. So there, smarty!

*(**Eddie** EXITS.)*

SAMANTHA: *(calling)* The new girl? Nellie? Nellie?

*(**Nellie** ENTERS, carrying a basket of laundry.)*

NELLIE: Yes, miss? Are you calling me, miss?

SAMANTHA: Are you Nellie?

NELLIE: Yes, miss.

SAMANTHA: *(excitedly)* Are you visiting the Rylands?

NELLIE: Oh no, miss. I'm working here.

SAMANTHA: *(eagerly)* Would you like to play with my doll Lydia and me?

NELLIE: Well, I'd like to. But I really can't.

SAMANTHA: *(rising from the bench)* Won't they let you?

NELLIE: No, I don't think so, miss. I've got my job to do.

SAMANTHA: *(laughing)* My name's Samantha. You don't have to call me "miss." I'll help you fold the laundry. Then we can play.

NELLIE: Oh, no, you shouldn't.

*(**Samantha** tucks her doll under her arm, takes Nellie's basket, and puts it on the ground.)*

SAMANTHA: Come on, we'll be done in a minute. Here, you'd better put Lydia on the bench.

*(**Samantha** hands the doll to Nellie. **Nellie** looks at the doll for a moment, then puts her on the bench. **Samantha** and **Nellie** sit down on the bench to fold the laundry.)*

SAMANTHA: Why are you working here?

NELLIE: My father works in a factory in the city, and my mother does washing. But there are three of us children, you see. Bridget, Jenny, and me. There wasn't enough food. And there wasn't enough coal. So I came here to work.

SAMANTHA: *(shocked)* You mean your parents sent you away? That's awful!

NELLIE: Oh, no. It's better here. It really is. Sometimes Mrs. Ryland scolds, and Eddie teases. He's bossy, too. *(proudly)* But I can earn a dollar a week and send it to my family for food. *(pausing)* That's not as much as I earned in the factory. But in the factory, the air was hot and dusty, and I started coughing a lot.

SAMANTHA: How terrible!

NELLIE: You see, it *is* better here. The air is good, and I get more food. *(sadly)* I just don't get to see my family much.

SAMANTHA: When do you go to school?

NELLIE: I've never been to school.

SAMANTHA: You've never been to school? Would you like to go?

NELLIE: *(eagerly)* Of course.

SAMANTHA: Nellie, I have an idea. We can meet here every day, and I will teach you. The Rylands won't miss you for just a little while, and I'll teach you everything—reading, arithmetic, writing, and geography. We'll have our own school!

NELLIE: Oh, that would be—

*(From OFFSTAGE, **Eddie** shouts.)*

EDDIE'S VOICE: NELLIEEEEEEEE!

NELLIE: *(jumping up)* I have to go! Good-bye!

*(**Nellie** EXITS, running, with the basket.)*

SAMANTHA: *(calling)* Good-bye! I'll wait for you here tomorrow! Good-bye, Nellie!

*(**Grandmary** ENTERS.)*

GRANDMARY: Here you are, Samantha! I've been looking for you. Your piano teacher is here.

SAMANTHA: *(rising)* Oh, I forgot about my lesson! *(excitedly)* Grandmary, I met the most wonderful new friend. Her name is Nellie, and she's going to live right next door. She's working at the Rylands'. We're going to do everything together!

GRANDMARY: *(firmly)* My dear, Nellie has a responsibility to the Rylands. You won't be a good friend to her if you keep her from her work. *(gently)* Do you understand?

SAMANTHA: Yes, Grandmary. *(picking up her doll)* I don't want Nellie to lose her job. But she's never been to school, and I promised I would teach her. Would that be wrong?

GRANDMARY: No, I suppose not. As long as it doesn't interfere with her work. Now come along. Your piano teacher is waiting.

*(**Samantha** and **Grandmary** EXIT.)*

ACT THREE

Scene: The lilac hedge, a few weeks later. Samantha and Nellie sit on the bench, giggling and talking as Nellie sews a rip in Lydia's skirt. There is a small jar half-full of beans sitting on the ground by Samantha.

SAMANTHA: And then we ran out of gas, so Uncle Gard had to push the car all the way home, and I had to steer it!

NELLIE: *(laughs, then coughs)* Was it fun?

SAMANTHA: Yes! Everything is fun with Uncle Gard.

NELLIE: Here, Lydia is all fixed.

*(**Nellie** hands the doll to Samantha. **Samantha** looks at the doll's skirt, then hugs the doll.)*

SAMANTHA: *(happily)* Thank you, Nellie. You're a good friend. Grandmary would have said I was careless if she had seen that rip in Lydia's skirt. Your stitches are so tiny and perfect!

NELLIE: Lydia is so beautiful, everything she has should be perfect.

SAMANTHA: *(nodding in agreement)* She is beautiful, isn't she? Before Lydia, and before you came, I was so lonely. There was nobody but Eddie.

*(**Samantha** and **Nellie** roll their eyes, shake their heads, and groan.)*

NELLIE: That Eddie!

SAMANTHA: Does he boss you a lot?

NELLIE: *(hiding a cough)* Sometimes.

SAMANTHA: If he gives you trouble, you tell me. I know how to take care of Eddie!

NELLIE: Well, he's in school all day, so—

SAMANTHA: *(breaking in)* School! I almost forgot! I brought some schoolwork for you today. Do you want to try it?

NELLIE: Yes!

*(**Samantha** sits on the ground. She spills beans from the jar onto the ground and arranges the beans in rows. **Nellie** picks up Lydia and gently studies her during the arithmetic lesson.)*

SAMANTHA: All right, Nellie, here are seven beans and here are five. Now, if you add them together—

NELLIE: *(breaking in)* Twelve.

SAMANTHA: Good! *(pausing to arrange more beans)* How about fourteen and nine?

NELLIE: *(without counting)* Twenty-three.

SAMANTHA: *(watching Nellie in surprise)* Seventeen and fifteen?

NELLIE: Thirty-two.

SAMANTHA: Jiminy! You're quick as lightning! Where did you learn arithmetic?

NELLIE: *(coughs)* Oh, I don't know. Lots of times in the city I did the shopping for Ma. I usually had about a dollar, and I had to get food for all of us. I had to know how many pennies things cost and how many pennies I had left, and I had to know fast. I guess that's how I learned to add and subtract in my head.

SAMANTHA: Well, you're awfully good at it!

NELLIE: *(sadly)* I wish I were good at being a maid. I try, but I'm just not strong enough. Yesterday I couldn't lift the laundry basket. Today I dropped Mrs. Ryland's breakfast tray. She said if she heard me cough one more time, she'd send me back to the city.

SAMANTHA: *(loudly)* No!

NELLIE: *(crouching down to put the beans back in the jar)* I can't help coughing. It seems like my cough keeps getting worse and worse.

SAMANTHA: *(helping Nellie)* That's because you're working so hard. You should be out in the sunshine, playing and having fun. You shouldn't be doing laundry or carrying breakfast trays for fat old Mrs. Ryland.

NELLIE: *(stands up quickly)* Samantha! You mustn't say that!

SAMANTHA: You shouldn't have to work at the Rylands'. I wish—

*(**Eddie** ENTERS. He jumps out from behind the hedge, teasing.)*

EDDIE: I see you, Samantha! I see you, Nellie! And you're really ugly. You're so ugly you'd scare a moose! You're so ugly—

SAMANTHA: *(breaking in)* Eddie, get out of here!

EDDIE: I'm telling. I'm telling on Samantha, and I'm telling on you, Nellie. I'm telling my mother you're playing with Samantha when you should be working. *(commanding)* Now you get back to the house.

SAMANTHA: *(stands up)* Eddie! Don't you dare order Nellie around! And if you tell anybody anything I will take your new pocket knife and I will stuff it full of taffy. Now go! And keep quiet!

EDDIE: *(mocking, singsong)* You can't make me! You can't make me!

SAMANTHA: *(firmly)* I know where your pocket knife is, Eddie.

EDDIE: You'll be sorry!

*(**Eddie** EXITS.)*

SAMANTHA: *(frustrated)* Oh, he makes me so MAD!

NELLIE: My pa would say that Eddie would pester the devil himself!

*(**Mrs. Ryland** ENTERS.)*

MRS. RYLAND: *(looking very stern)* Nellie! Come back to the house right now! This instant!

*(**Mrs. Ryland** turns away briskly and EXITS.)*

NELLIE: *(a little scared)* Yes, ma'am. I'm coming. *(hands the doll to Samantha)* I have to go, Samantha. Good-bye!

*(**Nellie** EXITS.)*

SAMANTHA: *(calling out, as she picks up the bean jar)* See you tomorrow!

ACT FOUR

Scene: The lilac hedge, the next afternoon.

*(**Uncle Gard** ENTERS. He yawns, lies down at the edge of the stage, and seems to go to sleep with his hat over his face.)*

*(**Nellie** ENTERS. She sits down and starts to cry softly. She doesn't see Uncle Gard.)*

*(**Samantha** ENTERS with her doll. She rushes over to Nellie and doesn't see Uncle Gard, either.)*

SAMANTHA: I'm sorry I'm late. I—Nellie! What's the matter?

NELLIE: *(crying)* They're sending me back to the city. Mrs. Ryland's driver is waiting for me now.

SAMANTHA: *(sitting down quickly)* What?

NELLIE: *(sadly)* Mrs. Ryland says I'm not strong enough to work for her, so she's sending me back.

SAMANTHA: *(comforting)* Oh, Nellie! Are you sick?

NELLIE: *(coughs)* No, I'm not sick. But I still cough sometimes, and Mrs. Ryland is afraid I'll get sick and be a bother.

SAMANTHA: *(worried)* But Nellie, will you have to go to work in the factory again? You *will* get sick if you go back there!

*(**Nellie** pats Samantha's shoulder as **Samantha** pats Nellie's.)*

NELLIE: It will be all right, Samantha. Really it will. Only I'll miss you so much.

SAMANTHA: *(almost crying)* What will I do without you, Nellie? You're my best friend!

NELLIE: *(sincerely)* And you're my best friend, too!

SAMANTHA: *(handing the doll to Nellie lovingly)* Here, Nellie. You take Lydia. She will be your friend.

NELLIE: *(hugging the doll)* Oh, Samantha! Thank you!

*(From OFFSTAGE, a horse whinnies and **Mrs. Ryland** calls.)*

MRS. RYLAND'S VOICE: Nellie! It's time to go! Hurry up!

NELLIE: Good-bye, Samantha!

*(**Nellie** and **Samantha** hug.)*

SAMANTHA: Good-bye, Nellie! *(sadly)* Good-bye.

*(**Nellie** EXITS, carrying the doll.)*

(From OFFSTAGE, the sound of a horse's hooves.)

*(**Samantha** sits down quietly. She looks very sad. **Grandmary** ENTERS. She sees Samantha, but not Uncle Gard.)*

GRANDMARY: Samantha, you don't have your doll today. Are you tired of her already?

SAMANTHA: *(earnestly)* No, Grandmary. No, I *(she hesitates)*...I lost her.

GRANDMARY: *(shocked)* You lost her? *(scolding)* My dear Samantha, how are you ever going to become a young lady? I try and I try to give you a proper sense of value. I've told you so many times—

*(As Grandmary speaks, **Uncle Gard** gets up and walks toward her.)*

UNCLE GARD: *(breaking in)* I think Sam's sense of value is just fine, Mother. She gave the doll to Nellie. Nellie had to go back to the city. I was resting here and I heard everything.

GRANDMARY: I see. *(She pauses, looks at Uncle Gard, and then takes Samantha's hand.)* Well, Samantha, you have done something good and kind. You have acted like a fine young lady. I am proud of you. You are a fine young lady, indeed.

*(**Samantha** hugs Grandmary.)*

SAMANTHA: Grandmary, we've *got* to help Nellie and her family. Their life in the city is terrible. They don't have enough food, and they don't have enough coal to stay warm. Can we help them? Please?

GRANDMARY: *(smiling)* Yes, Samantha, yes! *Your* actions have spoken louder than words. If you care enough to give up your doll, then I can surely do something, too. We will find a way to help Nellie's family. I promise.

ACT FIVE

Scene: Grandmary's parlor, a week or so later. Grandmary is having tea. Nellie is with her, but she is hidden from the audience by a chair.

*(**Samantha** ENTERS and curtsies. She looks sad. She does not see Nellie.)*

SAMANTHA: Good afternoon, Grandmary.

GRANDMARY: Come in, my dear. *(smiling)* You have company.

*(**Nellie** runs to hug Samantha as **Samantha** runs to hug Nellie.)*

SAMANTHA: *(excitedly)* Nellie! Oh, Nellie, it's you. It's really you! You've come back! Are you working at the Rylands' again?

NELLIE: *(happily)* Oh no. I'm somewhere much better. And it's because of your grandmother. She did it, Samantha. She talked to Mrs. Van Sicklen, and Mrs. Van Sicklen hired my whole family to come and work for her. And guess what? We get to live there! All of us! In the rooms over the carriage house. Isn't that wonderful?

SAMANTHA: Oh, Nellie! You'll live only two houses away. We can play every single day when I get home from school.

NELLIE: *(excitedly)* Samantha, I'm going to school, too. Mrs. Van Sicklen told your grandmother I could. What do you think of that?

SAMANTHA: That's wonderful! It's ALL wonderful! I'm so glad you're back, Nellie! And I can't wait to meet your parents, and Bridget and Jenny! *(taking Nellie's hand)* Let's go now!

(***Samantha*** *and* ***Nellie*** *start to leave, but* ***Samantha*** *stops suddenly to look at Grandmary.* ***Grandmary*** *smiles and nods.* ***Samantha*** *crosses the room to hug her.)*

SAMANTHA: Grandmary, thank you! Thank you for helping Nellie and her family. You said you would, and you did. Your actions spoke louder than words, too.

(***Samantha*** *and* ***Nellie*** *EXIT together.)*

(***Grandmary*** *smiles and sits calmly, drinking her tea.)*

Actions Speak Louder Than Words

A Play About Samantha

Putting on the Play

Contents

Play Summary

The play takes place in the summer of 1904, in a small town near New York City. Samantha Parkington is a nine-year-old orphan who lives with Grandmary, her wealthy and very proper grandmother. Although her life with Grandmary is very secure and comfortable, Samantha is a little lonely. But then Nellie moves in next door. Nellie has been hired to work as a servant at the Rylands', and she and Samantha immediately become best friends. When Nellie is forced to leave the Rylands' and return to the city, Samantha—and Grandmary—show that actions speak louder than words.

Samantha ❧ 1904

Samantha lived at a time when America was changing rapidly. Factories produced new and inexpensive goods for many Americans—especially wealthy people like Grandmary—but life was hard for those who worked in the factories.

THE CHARACTERS

HOW TO BECOME YOUR CHARACTER

Close your eyes and imagine that you are your character. Then practice walking, talking, and moving as you think your character would.

Your imagination is your best tool for a successful performance. If you don't have a stage or elaborate costumes or props, act as if you do!

SAMANTHA NELLIE

GRANDMARY

To prepare for your role, study your character description. Check the script to see what other characters say about or to your character. Use those statements as clues to how you should act.

Samantha is a nine-year-old orphan living with her wealthy grandmother. She looks and speaks like a proper young lady, but she is full of energy and ideas.

Nellie works as a servant at the house next door to Samantha's. She and Samantha become best friends. Nellie is also nine years old, but she is shy and somewhat quiet. Nellie still coughs from the dust she breathed while working in a factory.

Grandmary is Samantha's very proper grandmother. She is about 55 years old. She speaks slowly and clearly and has perfect posture. Grandmary is strict, but it's easy to see how much she loves Samantha.

Uncle Gard is Samantha's jolly and understanding uncle. He is about 25 years old. Uncle Gard likes newfangled things like automobiles. He also likes to joke, especially with Samantha—but he knows when to take her seriously, too.

UNCLE GARD

EDDIE RYLAND MRS. RYLAND

Eddie Ryland is the bratty boy who lives next door. He is a little younger than Samantha and Nellie. He likes to boss Nellie and pester Samantha—but he is a little afraid of Samantha.

Mrs. Ryland is Eddie's mother and Nellie's employer. She is a snob. Mrs. Ryland has a loud and scolding voice.

Four actors can perform *Actions Speak Louder Than Words* if one actor takes the parts of Grandmary and Mrs. Ryland and another actor takes the parts of Uncle Gard and Eddie.

IF YOU FORGET YOUR LINES . . .

If you forget your lines and can't hear the prompter, just think about what your character would say and then ***ad-lib*** *(say it in your own words).*

THE DIRECTOR

PRAISING THE ACTORS

One of your most important jobs as director is to praise the actors. Watch for good things that happen during rehearsals and make them part of the finished performance. The best praise is specific and sincere. Keep a notebook handy for your notes about things to remember and praise.

One of the director's jobs is to help an actor "get into character" by helping him or her imagine what it would be like to truly be that character. How would a character show joy or anger? For example, would one character show joy by laughing aloud while another smiled quietly? Would a character stamp her foot in anger or turn her back?

Encourage actors to practice walking and talking as their characters. How would the main character of the play walk? How would her voice change when she is happy or upset? Helping the actors find answers to these kinds of questions will create a more believable performance.

BLOCKING THE ACTION

As the director, you help the actors plan how to move when they are onstage. This is called *blocking the action,* and it usually takes place during rehearsal. The script sometimes tells the actors

how and when to move, but it is your job to give additional directions. You also give the actors little signs, or *cues,* about when to go onstage and offstage.

When you are blocking the action, try to use the whole stage. Important action should take place near the front of the stage, close to the audience.

Actors should face the audience most of the time when they're speaking, so the audience can see the actors' faces and hear their lines. But sometimes you might ask an actor to turn away to show sadness or rejection.

KEEPING THE PLAY MOVING

Keep the play moving by helping the actors *overlap* their lines. To overlap, an actor says her first word just as the actor before says her last word. Combine overlapping with occasional pauses to make the play more lively and natural.

DIRECTOR'S TIPS

- *Make sure that all actors speak clearly and loudly enough to be heard.*
- *Help the actors "get into character" by asking questions about what their characters are like.*
- *Remind the actors to relax as they say their lines. Using props will help them move naturally.*
- *Plan the action so that the audience can see the actors' faces.*
- *Remind the actors not to stand between other actors and the audience.*

THE CREW

MUSIC AND MOOD

Before the show and during set changes and intermissions, set the mood with music. ***Ragtime*** *was one popular kind of music in Samantha's time. This photo shows the cover of some ragtime songs for the piano. Player piano music or barbershop quartet songs would also create the mood of the early 1900s.*

Just before the play starts, the stagehand in charge of music can ***fade out*** *the music by gradually lowering the volume until it can no longer be heard.*

Plays are exciting because lots of people work together to make them happen. The people behind the scenes are known as *the crew*. Crew members may include stagehands, costume makers, makeup and hair stylists, ushers, and a prompter.

Stagehands create sets by finding, building, and painting scenery. They also change the scenery between acts and operate the curtain.

The *sound crew* creates sound effects and operates the sound system.

The *lights crew* operates the lighting system.

The *stage manager* works closely with the director to manage what happens onstage. He or she marks the script with every sound or light cue and all set changes, and then makes sure every cue comes on time.

The *property master* or *property mistress* is responsible for finding or making *properties*—or *props*—and for having the props ready at the right time and in the right place. That way, the actors have exactly what they need each time they go onstage.

Costume makers help the actors find or make costumes. *Makeup* and *hair stylists* help the actors put on makeup and style their hair or wigs.

The *prompter* follows the play line by line in a script book and whispers lines from offstage if an actor forgets them.

Ushers take tickets and lead the audience to their seats. They are sometimes in charge of getting playbills, programs, and tickets ready for the show.

At the end of the performance, everyone who helped put on the show should take a bow at the curtain call!

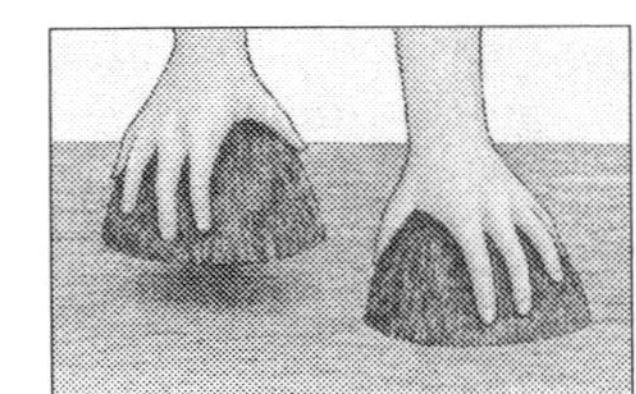

SOUND EFFECTS

During Act Four, a member of the sound crew can use coconut shells on a wooden table offstage or on the floor to make the sound of a horse walking. Practicing will help him or her know how fast or how loudly to "walk" the shells to make it sound real. Another crew member can make the sound of a whinnying horse.

The Costumes

Costume Tips

❧ *The very simplest way to identify characters doesn't even require costumes! An actor can wear a sign around his or her neck with the character's name printed large enough for the audience to read. This way, actors can easily switch parts without having to switch costumes!*

❧ *Make a pinafore or a work apron from an old white shirt worn backward. Cut off the sleeves and collar and make a square neckline by trimming the back of the shirt straight down an inch or two and then across the back of the shirt. Trim the shirt straight around the bottom. Left plain, the shirt can be Nellie's work apron. With ruffles or lace added, it can be Samantha's pinafore. Or make a pinafore by wearing a sundress over a long-sleeved dress.*

Costumes help bring a play to life and identify characters—but you can have a great performance without costumes, too!

Samantha's dress ends just below her knees, and she wears a puffy hair bow at the top of her head. She wears long white or black stockings and black high-button boots. Samantha covers her dress with a pinafore for play.

Nellie's clothes are not as nice as Samantha's. They are clean, but patched. Her boots and stockings are black. She wears a work apron over her dress, as shown here, except when she is a guest in Grandmary's parlor in Act Five. In Act Five, she also wears a puffy hair bow.

Grandmary wears a long, elegant skirt that reaches the floor and a blouse with a high collar. She might wear a pretty pin, such as a cameo, at the neck of her blouse.

Uncle Gard wears a suit, a white shirt, and a bow tie or a long tie. He has a mustache. He has a hat that he holds when he is inside and wears when he is outside.

Eddie Ryland wears *breeches*, or short pants, and a floppy bow tie. He wears black stockings and black or brown boots.

Mrs. Ryland dresses much like Grandmary. She wears a long skirt and a blouse with long sleeves and a high collar. She could also wear a jacket or a shawl.

Quick Changes

❧ *Practice making quick costume changes. Actors who play two characters change costumes twice, and must do so quickly!*

❧ *An actor playing both Grandmary and Mrs. Ryland can easily change costumes by adding a jacket or shawl when she is Mrs. Ryland.*

❧ *An actor playing both Uncle Gard and Eddie can wear a plain shirt and long, loose-fitting pants with rubber bands around each ankle under the cuffs. As Uncle Gard, the actor can add a suit jacket, clip-on tie, and hat. To change into Eddie's costume, the actor should remove the jacket, tie, and hat. Make Eddie's breeches by putting the rubber bands on top of the cuffs and pulling the pants up to just below the knee. "Blouse" the rest of each pant leg over the rubber band and around the knee, then add Eddie's floppy tie.*

STAGE SETS

SCENES

ACT ONE
Grandmary's parlor

ACT TWO
The lilac hedge between Grandmary's house and the Rylands' house

ACT THREE
The lilac hedge, a few weeks later

ACT FOUR
The lilac hedge, the next afternoon

ACT FIVE
Grandmary's parlor, a week later

You will need two sets for *Actions Speak Louder Than Words,* which has three outdoor scenes and two indoor scenes.

One way to create a background is by using large paper to make a mural. Light-brown paper across the back of your stage works best. Make cardboard cutouts that can stand out against the background mural. Use paint or chalk to add details on the cutouts and mural. Applying paint with a large sponge is fast and adds texture.

The lilac hedge could be painted as part of a mural. You could also make the hedge by using large pieces of cardboard that are taped to or leaned against a box, stool, or chair. Or you could make easel backs to support them, as shown. Paint the cardboard with green and purple paint to look like lilac bushes. Another way to make

bushes is with crumpled brown paper bags that are partly filled with crumpled newspapers. Paint them lightly first with green and then purple paint, and arrange several together to create bigger or higher bushes. When you make the hedge, be sure to leave a hole in the middle for the passageway between Samantha's and Eddie's yards.

LIGHTING

Lights help set the mood. Acts One and Five take place indoors. Soft lighting from one or two lamps on the stage or set will make it seem like indoors. Acts Two, Three, and Four take place outside. Use bright lighting that will suggest a sunny day.

Acts One and Five.

Acts Two, Three, and Four.

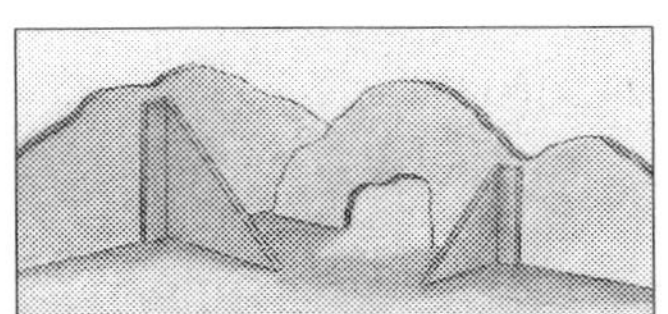

Make an easel back by taping a cardboard triangle to the back of the lilac bushes.

Props

Props

❧

ACT ONE
A teapot
Three cups and saucers
A plate of biscuits
A partly finished sampler
A doll in a fancy box

•

ACT TWO
A basket of laundry

•

ACT THREE
The doll
A needle and thread
A jar of beans

•

ACT FOUR
A man's straw hat
The doll

•

ACT FIVE
The doll
A teapot
Cups and saucers

Here are some ideas for making or finding the props for this play.

A silver teapot would look lovely, but a toy tea set would work, too. Use cookies or crackers for the biscuits. A *sampler* is a piece of fabric with embroidered letters stitched on it. Use a piece of light-colored material for the sampler, and with a marker, print part of the phrase "Actions Speak Louder Than Words" on the fabric.

You can use a real doll or a stuffed animal if you don't have a doll.

A medium-size peanut butter or mayonnaise jar filled halfway will hold enough beans for the counting lesson. Use large uncooked beans, such as lima beans or kidney beans—they are easier to see and handle than small beans!

The Stage

There are special terms to describe the front, back, and sides of the stage. These terms were used by actors and directors long ago, and are still used today.

Stages used to be built on a slant, with the back part of the stage higher than the front. This angle allowed the audience to see the actors better. The terms *upstage* and *downstage* come from the way the stage slanted. *Upstage* is the area farthest from the audience—the area that used to be higher. *Downstage* is the front of the stage, nearest the audience. An actor standing in the exact middle of the stage is at *center stage*.

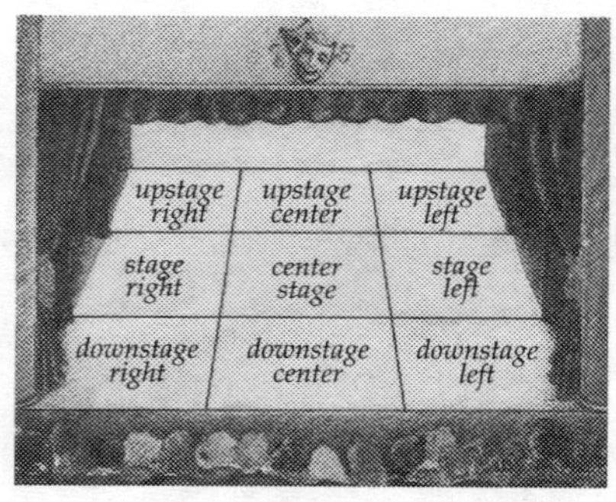

When an actor stands at center stage, facing the audience, the area to the actor's right is *stage right* and the area to the actor's left is *stage left*. The best way to remember *stage right* and *stage left* is to face the audience.

MUSTACHES AND BOWS

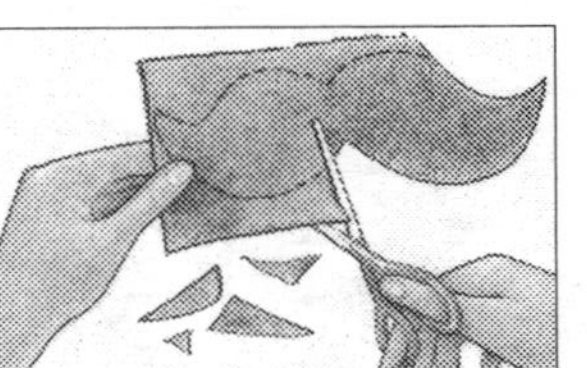

A PAPER MUSTACHE
You can use masking tape or Scotch tape to attach your paper mustache.

A MAKEUP MUSTACHE
Rub a little cold cream above your lip before drawing the mustache. If you do, it'll come off more easily when you're ready to remove it!

MAKING MUSTACHES

Make a paper mustache by cutting a shape like that shown and have the actor tape it in place. Make it from brown or black construction paper, or color it with a brown or black crayon or pen.

For a makeup mustache, use a brown or black eyebrow pencil to make short, slightly curved lines between the nose and the upper lip. This kind of mustache stays on better than a paper one, but is more difficult to remove if one actor plays both Uncle Gard and Eddie.

For quick changes, keep tissues, cold cream, and the eyebrow pencil backstage. At the end of Act One, if the actor playing Uncle Gard also plays Eddie, he or she should quickly smear cold cream over the mustache and wipe it off with a tissue. The actor will have to quickly reapply the mustache again at the end of Act Three, because Uncle Gard is back onstage right at the beginning of Act Four.

MAKING HAIR BOWS

For Samantha's and Nellie's hair bows, you can use large, ready-made hair bows or make your own. To make a large hair bow like those worn in Samantha's time, use a piece of ribbon 2 to 3 inches wide and about 1 yard long. The wider your ribbon is, the fuller your bow will be. Tie it as shown, and make the ends even with each other and the same length as the two looped parts. Use your fingers to shape the loops so that they are full and puffy, just like Samantha's. A barrette or hairpins will hold the bow in place.

MAKING A PUFFY BOW
Don't tie your bow too tightly—it will be prettier if it's a little loose. Use your fingers to spread the ribbon out to make it full and puffy.

★ WAR ON THE HOME FRONT ★

WORLD WAR TWO AMERICA—1944

MOLLY ★ 1944

During World War Two, Americans on the home front worried about loved ones fighting overseas. And they had to learn to get by with less of just about everything. But Americans were patriotic and pitched in together to help the war effort.

ABOUT THE PLAY

War on the Home Front is a play about nine-year-old Molly McIntire, a fictional girl growing up on the home front during World War Two. She lives in the fictional city of Jefferson, Illinois. Like many Americans, Molly's father is overseas, and Molly misses him very much.

Although World War Two was being fought far away, it brought changes to life on the home front. Families were separated because so many Americans were fighting overseas. Women started working in factories and offices or doing volunteer work to support the war effort. Many goods and foods were sent to soldiers overseas and became scarce at home.

In *War on the Home Front,* it is just before Halloween and Molly is planning her Halloween costume. But wartime shortages are making it difficult to find good costumes. As Molly and her two best friends, Linda and Susan, discuss their costumes, Molly's brother Ricky starts to pester and tease them. When he refuses to stop, Molly and her friends find a way to embarrass him.

But Ricky strikes back and ruins their costumes. The girls seek revenge—and war nearly breaks out at home.

Reading and dramatizing *War on the Home Front* will help your students understand what life was like for children on the home front during World War Two. Wartime shortages were frustrating to everyone, perhaps especially to children. With their mothers working outside the home and their fathers far away, children had to learn to be more resourceful in many ways. The related activity will help your students think about some of the things that Molly and Ricky—and many others—experienced during the war. This firsthand experience will help them approach the play with greater understanding, both as performers and as members of the audience.

Historical Context

World War Two began long before the United States entered the war in 1941. Led by Adolf Hitler, the Nazi Party of Germany had built a war economy during the 1930s and started attacking other European countries—first Poland in September 1939, then Belgium, France, and England. The Nazis attacked the Soviet Union as well. Germany eventually formed an alliance as the Axis Powers with Italy, Spain, and Japan.

America maintained its longtime isolationist stance while the Nazis cut through Europe and the Japanese invaded China and Korea. Although America contributed arms and supplies to the Allied forces of England, France, and the Soviet Union, most Americans did not want to fight in a war overseas. But when Japanese planes bombed an American military base in Pearl Harbor on December 7, 1941, America's Congress declared war on Japan. Japan's allies then declared war on the United States, and America went to war in both Europe and the Pacific. Once the United States entered the war, thousands of Americans volunteered to fight or serve as mechanics, drivers, nurses, and doctors in the United States Armed Forces.

As the German army crossed Europe, the Nazis forced Europe's Jewish people into concentration camps—along with gypsies, political dissidents, and others the Nazis deemed "undesirable." There, they were used for slave labor and many were immediately killed. Altogether, about six million Jews died. Most Americans were unaware of the concentration camps until near the end of the war, when the camps were liberated by Allied forces.

Americans at home adjusted to wartime shortages and other hardships of war. People thought of themselves as "fighting on the home front." They contributed in many ways: by collecting and recycling scrap metal, planting Victory gardens, and doing volunteer work. Women went to work in offices and factories, where they ran businesses and built planes and ships.

Germany finally surrendered on May 7, 1945, and the war in Europe ended. The war in the Pacific ended on September 2, 1945, after the United States dropped atomic bombs on Nagasaki and Hiroshima. American soldiers and war workers came home, and families like the McIntires were reunited. Many women gave up their

Home Front Pastimes

Movies were popular during the war, and children saved their money for the Saturday matinee. Before the movie started, there were always cartoons—and a newsreel about the war. Movies about the war were so popular that Hollywood produced more than 500 war films between 1942 and 1945.

*On the stage, comedies, patriotic plays about the war, and musicals were favorites. The musical **Oklahoma!** was first performed in 1943.*

Women at Work

Six million women joined the labor force during World War Two. As men left their jobs to enter the armed forces, women were hired to replace them. At least two million women worked in heavy industry and more went to work in offices.

When men come home at the end of the war, women workers left or were fired so men would have their jobs back. Although many women were happy to return home, others wanted to continue working—but posters and magazine articles told them that it was patriotic to give the jobs back to the men.

RADIO IN THE 1940S

The radio was important to American families in Molly's time. Families often listened to the radio together, as some families do with television today. Musical performances, quiz shows, comedies, and dramas were popular, and newscasts were an important source of information.

wartime jobs so that returning soldiers could have their jobs back. Although peace had been reestablished, the atomic bombs that had ended the war were so powerful that many feared the world would never be truly safe again. In 1945, the United Nations was created in the hope that the world would not go to war again.

THEMES IN THE PLAY

War on the Home Front could be used in social studies units about World War Two, or in any thematic unit about war. The play would also fit well in thematic units about change, families, shortages and recycling, conflict and conflict resolution, and cooperation.

AFTER PERFORMING—A RADIO TALK SHOW

RADIO TALK SHOW

Objectives:
To examine issues related to mothers working outside the home

To dramatize people with differing points of view, and to speak from those points of view

Teacher's Role: *Participant, as a talk show host*

Student Roles: *Guests or studio audience members interested in the topic of mothers working outside the home*

Time Needed: *25 minutes*

Space Needed: *Desks or chairs arranged to simulate a talk show in a studio*

Materials Needed: *Index cards, name tags, and a pretend microphone (optional)*

This activity may be most effective after reading or performing *War on the Home Front.* It will allow students to explore in a fun and dramatic way issues related to mothers working outside the home.

Radio interviews and discussions were common in the 1940s, but "talk shows" like those on television today didn't really exist in Molly's time. However, many of your students may be familiar with today's talk shows. You can use the talk show format to explore issues about working mothers—something common during World War Two and common today. As students consider the issue as it relates to Molly and her family, they will probably be able to draw from their own experience.

Context

The war is ending, and Dad is due home soon. Molly expects that everything will be "normal" again. But when Mom decides she wants to continue working at the Red Cross, Molly and her siblings are upset. They—and many others—don't understand why Mrs. McIntire would want to keep her job. Mrs. McIntire has tried to explain that it makes her feel good about herself to have a job at which she excels, to contribute to the family's income, and to have interests outside the family.

Directions

1. Prepare materials and set the scene: Arrange the space to look like a radio studio: place six chairs around a microphone in front of the "studio audience."

Prepare index cards with the photocopied guest profiles on page 155: Molly, Ricky, Mrs. McIntire, a returning soldier who wants Mrs. McIntire's job, Mrs. McIntire's boss at the Red Cross, and a psychologist. The other important role is that of the talk show host, which you will play. Make up a name and personality for yourself that you feel comfortable dramatizing.

You can also create profiles for audience members, such as the McIntires' housekeeper, another psychologist, and other returning soldiers, working women, and children.

2. Assign roles: Ask six students to play the parts of the guests. Give them a few minutes away from the class to think about and prepare their roles. Encourage them to read the information on the other cards so that they have a broad understanding of the points of view of the other guests. Meanwhile, talk to the audience members about other points of view. Explain that you will be the show host and that they are expected to listen, ask questions, or make comments in role when invited to do so.

3. The broadcast: Go into role. Welcome the studio and radio audiences and introduce your topic: mothers who want to continue working outside the home even though the war is ending. Describe the McIntire family's situation as an example of what many families may be experiencing. Then invite the guests to enter in any order you'd like—either all at once, or one at a time so you can introduce and talk to them. Invite the audience to participate in the discussion. Ask tough questions and encourage the audience to do so. Continue as long as the discussion remains focused. Conclude the talk show by thanking your guests, audience, and sponsors.

4. Reflection and discussion: Ask everyone to come out of role. Encourage additional discussion about what was said during the activity. Was there anything that perhaps should have been brought up during the talk show but wasn't? Is it fair to ask women who helped win the war by working to give up their jobs to returning soldiers? Is Mrs. McIntire being unpatriotic or "unnatural" for wanting to work? If a mother works, does that mean she doesn't care about her children? How will women whose husbands were killed or injured support their families if they lose their jobs? What about women like the McIntires' housekeeper, who'll lose her job if Mrs. McIntire stays home? Could some of the returning soldiers take care of the children? How is the McIntires' situation similar to or different from life today?

Make a Microphone

Make or find a microphone. A tennis or Ping-Pong ball stuck to the top of a toilet paper tube works well. You can cover it with tinfoil or paint it black to make it look more realistic. You could also add a card with the radio station call letters on the front of the microphone.

Commercial Breaks

Go to a commercial if you need to clarify your expectations of the audience or guests, or to give everyone a break or a chance to think quietly.

If you have a commercial break, be sure to mention the show's sponsors and products from the 1940s—or encourage the radio audience to buy War Bonds to support the war effort.

Radio Research

In preparation for the talk show, ask some of your students to research the sponsors of radio shows in the 1940s and the products they advertised. Encourage them to write and perform a short ad for a commercial break.

Other students might want to look for actual recordings of 1940s radio broadcasts to share with the class.

War on the Home Front

A Play About Molly

★

Play Script

TIPS FOR ACTORS

★ Use your imagination. If you don't have a fancy stage or elaborate props and costumes, act as if you do!

★ Speak clearly and loudly enough to be heard. Don't turn your back to the audience or stand between another actor and the audience.

★ Pretend that you **are** the character you are playing. If you forget your lines and can't hear the prompter, think about what the character would really say and say it in your own words.

★ Act and speak at the same time. Directions before your lines will tell you things to do as you are saying those lines. For example,

> *(**Molly** and **Susan** are doing the hula.)*
>
> **MOLLY:** This was a wonderful Halloween!

★ Other directions make suggestions about how to say a line. For example,

> **MOLLY:** *(angrily)* Ricky, I'll get you for this!

★ Cooperate with the director and the other actors. And don't forget to smile at the curtain call!

WAR ON THE HOME FRONT

A Play About Molly

CHARACTERS

MOLLY
A lively nine-year-old girl who is growing up on America's home front during World War Two

LINDA
One of Molly's best friends, a practical schemer who is also nine years old

SUSAN
Molly's other best friend, who is nine years old and a cheerful dreamer

RICKY
Molly's pesty twelve-year-old brother

DOLORES
The glamorous high school girl Ricky has a crush on

MOM
Molly's mother, who holds the family together while Dad is away taking care of wounded soldiers

The action takes place one Halloween during World War Two, in the McIntire family's backyard.

ACT ONE

Scene: A sunny fall afternoon in the McIntires' backyard. Ricky is bouncing his basketball in the driveway.

*(**Molly, Linda,** and **Susan** ENTER. They are carrying schoolbooks, and **Susan** is eating an apple. **Molly, Linda,** and **Susan** sit on the back steps. **Ricky** groans.)*

LINDA: I wish you hadn't bragged about our Halloween costumes, Molly.

MOLLY: I didn't brag. I just said they were a *secret*.

LINDA: Yeah, well, they're a secret to *us*, too. Halloween is tomorrow, and we don't even know what we're going to be yet. And it's going to be tough this year. Things like Halloween costumes are hard to get because of the war.

MOLLY: *(confidently)* Don't worry. We'll think of something.

LINDA and **SUSAN:** Like what?

MOLLY: *(speaking slowly, as if she's just had this idea)* Well, how about Cinderella and the two ugly—I mean the two stepsisters?

*(**Ricky** grabs his neck, sticks out his tongue, and acts as if he's choking. The girls look annoyed, then ignore him.)*

SUSAN: Oooooh! Cinderella!

LINDA: Who gets to be Cinderella?

MOLLY: *(quickly)* We don't have to decide that right away. Let's . . . uh . . . let's wait and see who has the best ball dress, and that's the one who will be Cinderella. The other two will be stepsisters.

LINDA: I don't think it's fair. Who wants to be an ugly stepsister?

RICKY: *(joking)* You're all ugly step *sitters* today. Get it?

MOLLY: *(glaring at him)* Cut it out, Ricky.

SUSAN: I think Cinderella is a good idea. What dress would you wear, Molly?

*(As **Molly** describes the dress, **Ricky** smiles a sickly-sweet smile and flutters his eyelids. He pretends to put a crown on his head when Molly describes the star crown. He rubs his sleeves as she describes the fluffy angora top. He pretends he's wearing a full skirt as she describes the long, floaty skirt of her dream costume. He holds up his sneakered foot as she describes the glass slippers. **Molly, Linda,** and **Susan** try to ignore Ricky, but it is clear that he is annoying them.)*

MOLLY: *(dreamily)* Well, I'd have a crown with shiny silver stars on my head. The top of the dress would be made of fluffy white angora. The skirt would be long and floaty. It would be made of pink silk, with silver stars to match the crown. And I'd have tiny glass slippers on my feet, of course.

LINDA: Gosh, Molly, your costume sounds great. But...uh, does it really exist? I mean, do you actually *have* it?

MOLLY: Well...no, not yet.

LINDA: Because, well, I'm sorry to say this, but I don't think anybody can get glass slippers or material like angora and silk now, because of the war.

MOLLY: But if I could—

LINDA: *(breaking in)* Even if you *could*, it would be wrong to use the material for something impractical like a Halloween costume. It would be unpatriotic and wasteful. And I bet your mom is too busy with her war work for the Red Cross to make any ball dresses.

MOLLY: *(sighing)* I guess you're right. I guess we'll have to forget Cinderella until after the war.

SUSAN: Anyway, it would be more fun if we were all exactly the same thing, like the Three Musketeers or the Three Blind Mice.

RICKY: *(loudly)* You'd be perfect as the Three Little Pigs. Or you could be the Three Bears. How about the Three Stooges? Or the Three Kings of Orient?

MOLLY: *(angrily)* That's *enough*, Ricky.

*(**Ricky** sings in a loud, teasing voice. **Molly** yells while he sings.)*

RICKY: We three kings of Orient are,
Tried to smoke a rubber cigar,
It was loaded, it exploded....

MOLLY: STOP IT!!!

*(**Ricky** stops suddenly. He bounces the basketball under his legs and behind his back. He twirls the ball on the tip of one finger. **Molly, Linda,** and **Susan** look to see if someone is coming.)*

LINDA: How come Ricky stopped teasing us? Who is he showing off for?

MOLLY: I don't see anybody but Jill and her new friend Dolores. See, they're talking at the end of the driveway.

SUSAN: Gosh, Dolores sure is pretty! She looks like a movie star!

RICKY: *(calling in an odd, squeaky voice)* Hi, Dolores . . .

*(**Ricky** turns, jumps, and shoots the basketball. **Molly, Linda,** and **Susan** look at one another and giggle.)*

MOLLY: Ricky has a crush on Dolores!

RICKY: I do not!

MOLLY, LINDA, and **SUSAN:** *(chanting loudly)*
Ricky and Dolores up in a tree,
K-I-S-S-I-N-G!
First comes love,
Then comes marriage,
Then comes Ricky with a baby carriage!

*(**Ricky** throws the basketball at them. **Molly** catches it.)*

RICKY: Cut it out!

MOLLY, LINDA, and **SUSAN:** Ricky has a crush! Ricky loves Dolores!

MOLLY: Hi-i-i, Do-lor-esss!

*(**Molly, Linda,** and **Susan** tease Ricky. They chant, make loud kissing noises, and imitate his squeaky voice. **Molly** pretends to kiss the basketball.)*

LINDA and **SUSAN:** Eeeeeuuuuwwww!

*(**Ricky** shakes his fist at the girls.)*

RICKY: You'll be sorry! You'll pay for this! I'll get you!

*(**Ricky** EXITS.)*

LINDA: Gee, he really sounds mad.

MOLLY: Well, he started it. He wouldn't stop teasing us. Come on. I think my mom is home. Let's go ask her if she has any good ideas for costumes.

*(**Molly, Linda,** and **Susan** EXIT, singing softly, "Ricky and Dolores up in a tree.")*

ACT TWO

Scene: Halloween evening, the McIntires' backyard.

*(**Linda, Susan,** and **Molly** ENTER. They are dressed in hula dancer costumes and carry bags of Halloween treats. **Linda** is singing a Hawaiian song. **Molly** and **Susan** are doing the hula.)*

MOLLY: This was a wonderful Halloween!

*(**Linda** sits on the steps to sort her treats. **Molly** keeps doing the hula. **Susan** eats a popcorn ball.)*

SUSAN: Mmm-hmm. *(happily)* Your mom's idea about being hula dancers was great. Everybody loved our costumes.

LINDA: I didn't get as many cookies or candies as last year.

MOLLY: *(explaining)* People don't have any sugar to spare from their rations.

LINDA: Yes, but I still got a lot of really good stuff—apples, doughnuts, peanuts, molasses kisses, popcorn balls...

MOLLY: Remember how the Pedersens asked us to do a hula before they gave us some cider? That was fun. I like the way our grass skirts make a swishing sound when we dance. They're so graceful and pretty.

LINDA: Remember, your mom wants to take a picture of us before we change.

MOLLY: *(sadly, as she stops dancing)* She wants to send the picture to Dad, so he won't miss seeing our Halloween this year even though he's away at the war.

*(**Susan** spins around to make her skirt twirl out.)*

SUSAN: *(comforting)* Well, I think these costumes are so beautiful, we should be really careful and save them. Then we can use them again next year.

MOLLY: Yes, they *are* good costumes. Maybe we *should* save them for next year. But now I guess we'd better go in. I'm sorry Halloween is over. It was such a wonderful—

*(**Molly** is interrupted by a huge splash of water. From OFFSTAGE, a hose sprays straight at the girls. **Molly, Linda,** and **Susan** jump up to get away from the water, but they are soaked.)*

MOLLY, LINDA, and **SUSAN:** AHHHHHH! Stop the water! Stop! My costume! Stop!

*(The water stops. **Molly, Linda,** and **Susan** are dripping wet. Their costumes are in shreds. Their paper flowers are flattened and torn. Their treats are scattered everywhere in soggy lumps. **Linda** gasps and sputters, **Susan** sobs, and **Molly** is almost crying.)*

MOLLY: Ruined! My costume is completely wrecked by that water! Who would spray us with a hose like that? Who did this?

*(From OFFSTAGE in a low, slow, steady voice, **Ricky** sings.)*

RICKY'S VOICE:
I see London,
I see France,
I can see your underpants!

MOLLY, LINDA, and **SUSAN:** Ricky!

MOLLY: *(angrily)* Ricky, I'll get you for this! You ruined our costumes with that hose! You'll be sorry—you wait! You'll be *really* sorry!

LINDA: That mean old Ricky! Look at us! I'm sopping wet!

SUSAN: I'm wet, too! And I'm freezing!

MOLLY: *(taking charge)* You go inside, Susan. Linda and I will clean up this mess.

*(**Susan** EXITS.)*

(***Linda*** *and* ***Molly*** *try to clean up the mess.)*

LINDA: I knew Ricky was mad at us, but I didn't know he was *that* mad. Are you going to tell your mom?

MOLLY: No, I'm not a tattletale. Besides, she'll be too easy on him. *(angrily)* We have to fix Ricky ourselves. We've got to teach him a lesson he'll never forget.

LINDA: How?

MOLLY: I don't know. *(determinedly)* But I'll think of something to make him really sorry.

(***Mom*** *ENTERS from the house.)*

MOM: Molly! What on earth happened? What happened to your costumes? And your bags of treats?

MOLLY: Uh, well, Mom, they got wet.

MOM: Well, I can see *that*. How did they get wet?

LINDA: *(to Mom)* By a hose. Ricky—

MOLLY: *(breaking in)* We walked into a hose. By mistake.

MOM: Who would be using a hose on a windy Halloween night?

MOLLY: Just someone.

MOM: *(warning)* Molly McIntire, I have the distinct feeling that I am not being told the whole story. Ricky! Ricky, come here!

(***Ricky*** *ENTERS. He is dressed as a pirate.)*

MOM: Perhaps you can tell me what happened, Ricky.

RICKY: *(in a squeaky, guilty voice)* Me? I didn't… I mean…I mean…

MOM: Go on, Ricky.

RICKY: Well, it was just a joke, Mom. Just a joke on the girls. You know, a Halloween joke? *(holds out his trick-or-treat bag)* Trick or treat?

LINDA: A mean trick.

MOM: What did you do?

RICKY: *(closing his trick-or-treat bag)* I just got a little water on their costumes.

MOLLY: *(angrily)* A *little* water? You sprayed tons and tons of water all over us, Ricky!

LINDA: You squirted us with a *hose*!

MOLLY: You ruined our costumes and all our treats!

MOM: Is that true?

LINDA and **MOLLY:** Yes!

MOM: Ricky?

*(**Ricky** looks at his feet.)*

RICKY: Yes, ma'am.

MOM: Ricky, that was a very mean thing to do. I'm ashamed of you, treating your sister and her friends that way. I think I can say that your father would be ashamed of you, too. I'm going to punish you just as I think he would punish you. You are to apologize to these girls. Then you are to give your bag of Halloween treats to Linda, Molly, and Susan to share. You may keep one treat, and only one, for yourself. Is that clear?

RICKY: Yes, ma'am.

MOM: All right. Go ahead.

*(**Ricky** shoves his bag of treats at Molly and mutters an apology.)*

RICKY: Sorry.

MOM: Let's go in now. No more fighting.

*(**Molly, Ricky, Linda,** and **Mom** EXIT quietly.)*

ACT THREE

Scene: The next morning, in the McIntires' backyard. Linda, Susan, and Molly sit on the back steps, dividing Ricky's bag of treats.

LINDA: You were right, Molly. Your mom was way too easy on Ricky. Except for when she said your father would be ashamed of Ricky, too.

SUSAN: Yeah! Ricky wrecked our Halloween, and he's hardly suffering at all.

MOLLY: Well, we'll just have to think up a plan to make Ricky *really* suffer. This is war!

SUSAN: Let's let the air out of his bicycle tires.

MOLLY: No, that's not bad enough.

LINDA: We could put frogs under his pillow. Dozens and dozens of frogs!

SUSAN: Yeah, but then *we'd* have to catch the frogs.

MOLLY, LINDA, and **SUSAN:** Eeeeeuuuuwwww!

SUSAN: *(rising and pretending to phone)* We could disguise our voices and call him up on the telephone. We could pretend we're his teacher and say he has to stay after school every day next week for being bad.

MOLLY: No. That's no good. It doesn't embarrass him in front of anybody. We have to really embarrass him in front of lots of people, or in front of someone he'd hate to be embarrassed in front of. Like Mom, or—

LINDA: *(breaking in)* Or Dolores!

MOLLY: Yes, that's it! Embarrass him in front of Dolores!

SUSAN: But how? *(sits down again)* We can't squirt him with a hose so that his underwear shows.

MOLLY: *(slowly, thinking out loud)* Wait a minute! Dolores...underwear...I think I have a plan, but all three of us have to cooperate or it won't work.

SUSAN: We'll cooperate!

LINDA: We'll do it!

MOLLY: Good! Okay, let's see. Linda, you distract Mom. Keep her inside. Susan, you come inside with me. When I give you the signal, tell Dolores her boyfriend wants to see her outside.

SUSAN: *(protesting)* But that's *lying*.

MOLLY: *(firmly)* Susan, we're at *war* with Ricky. During a war you don't worry about a little lie here or there. Do you want to get back at Ricky or not?

SUSAN: Well, yes. But…

MOLLY: No excuses in a war! You've *got* to do it. Ready? Let's go!

*(**Molly, Linda,** and **Susan** EXIT.)*

*(**Ricky** ENTERS. He shoots baskets for a moment or two.)*

*(**Molly** and **Susan** ENTER. They wait at the edge of the stage with a big paper bag stuffed with dirty laundry. Ricky doesn't see them. He continues to shoot baskets.)*

*(**Dolores** ENTERS from the other side.)*

DOLORES: Hi, Ricky!

*(**Ricky** turns to say hello. **Molly** and **Susan** yell as loudly as they can. They fling everything in the bag onto Ricky and Dolores. Underwear, T-shirts, and socks fill the air.)*

*(**Molly** and **Susan** EXIT, still yelling.)*

*(**Dolores** screeches and lifts some undershorts off her head with the tips of her fingers.)*

DOLORES: *(looking at the undershorts)* What's this?

*(From OFFSTAGE, **Molly** and **Susan** sing.)*

MOLLY'S and **SUSAN'S VOICES:**
I see London,
I see France,
Those are Ricky's underpants!

*(**Ricky** races around frantically, gathering up his underwear.)*

(***Dolores** laughs and shakes her head in a very grown-up way. She hands Ricky his undershorts.*)

DOLORES: Here, Ricky. I believe these cute little underpants belong to you. Sort of a disgusting and childish joke for you to play, don't you think?

RICKY: *(sputtering)* But, but I didn't, but I...

(***Dolores** EXITS.*)

(***Molly** ENTERS.*)

MOLLY: There's YOUR Halloween trick or treat, Ricky!

(***Ricky** shakes a fist full of underwear at Molly.*)

RICKY: YOU! You did this! I'll get you! You'll be sorry! This is really *war*! I'll—

(***Ricky** stops suddenly.*)

(***Mom** ENTERS. She is very angry.*)

MOM: Molly! Ricky! Come here.

(***Molly** and **Ricky** face Mom. They are ashamed. **Mom** is quiet for a moment. Then she speaks in a tired, sad voice.*)

MOM: I suppose these tricks you've been playing on each other don't seem very serious to you. But they are mean, childish, and wasteful. I'm disappointed in you, but more than that, I'm sad and discouraged. If we can't get along together, who can?

(***Molly** and **Ricky** look at each other, then look at their feet. **Mom** continues.*)

MOM: This fighting has to stop. This is exactly what starts wars—this meanness, anger, and revenge. Two sides decide to get even and end up hurting everyone. I won't have any more of it in our house. Is that understood?

MOLLY and **RICKY:** *(mumbling)* Yes, ma'am.

MOM: All right. Until there are no more tricks in this house, there will be no more treats. Ricky, you will spend the day raking the yard. Make sure you clean up the mess you made last night. Molly, you and your friends will spend the day doing Ricky's laundry. I want everything washed, hung out to dry, folded, and put away. That's it. Get to work.

*(**Mom** EXITS.)*

*(**Molly** and **Ricky** pick up the remaining underwear.)*

MOLLY: *(quietly)* Ricky, give me your under—uh, your things.

*(**Ricky** hands her the bundle.)*

RICKY: Here. I think that's all of them.

MOLLY: Okay, thanks. Uh, listen, we didn't—I mean, we didn't want to keep fighting with you, exactly. We were just mad, and the fight kept getting bigger and bigger. We only wanted to embarrass you. We shouldn't have done it. I'm sorry. I really am.

RICKY: It's okay. I guess I deserved it. Your trick was mean, but you know, it was funny, too.

MOLLY: Yeah?

RICKY: Yeah. *(sincerely)* I'm kind of glad not to be fighting against you anymore. You three have pretty good ideas, even if you are a bunch of triple dips. I guess it's better to be on your side than to be your enemy.

MOLLY: Thanks, Ricky. I'm glad our war is over. I think it's much better to be friends.

RICKY: You know what? With all that laundry, you look like Cinderella—*before* the ball.

MOLLY: *(laughing)* Yeah, that's right. So it seems like I sort of got to be Cinderella for Halloween after all!

*(**Molly** and **Ricky** EXIT.)*

War on the Home Front

A Play About Molly

★

Putting on the Play

Contents

Play Summary

The play takes place late one October in the middle of World War Two, in Molly McIntire's backyard. Nine-year-old Molly and her best friends Linda and Susan dream of the perfect Halloween, but they know that wartime shortages will make it hard for them to find good costumes. Molly's mom isn't home to help them because of her job at the Red Cross—and Molly's dad is overseas taking care of wounded soldiers.

When Molly's older brother Ricky keeps hanging around and teasing them, the girls find a way to embarrass him. Ricky strikes back, and the girls plan revenge—until war nearly breaks out on the home front.

Molly ★ 1944

During World War Two, Americans on the home front worried about loved ones fighting overseas. And they had to learn to get by with less of just about everything. But Americans were patriotic and pitched in together to help the war effort.

THE CHARACTERS

HOW TO BECOME YOUR CHARACTER

★ *Close your eyes and imagine that you are your character. Then practice walking, talking, and moving as you think your character would.*

★ *Your imagination is your best tool for a successful performance. If you don't have a stage or elaborate costumes or props, act as if you do!*

MOLLY

LINDA

SUSAN

To prepare for your role, study your character description. Check the script to see what other characters say about or to your character. Use those statements as clues to how you should act.

Molly is nine years old and has dreams of being elegant and glamorous. She is optimistic and energetic. Molly has ideas for just about everything—from perfect Halloween costumes to revenge on Ricky.

Linda is one of Molly's two best friends. She is nine years old. She is practical, realistic, and brisk, and wants things to work. She goes along with Molly's schemes, but she asks questions first.

Susan is Molly's other best friend. She is also nine years old. She sometimes wonders if the girls' plans are right, but she is easier to convince than Linda is. She is enthusiastic, but quieter than Molly and Linda.

Ricky is Molly's 12-year-old brother, who likes to tease Molly and her friends. He also likes basketball—and Dolores. Ricky is a bit of a show-off. He has a temper, especially when other people find out about his secret crush on Dolores.

RICKY

DOLORES

MOM

Dolores is 14 years old and a friend of Molly's sister Jill. She is glamorous and grown-up, and is one of the most popular girls in high school.

Mom holds the McIntire family together. She is firm but loving. She is patient and understanding, but she has her limits. She wants the war overseas to end—as well as the war at home between Molly and Ricky.

Four actors can present *War on the Home Front* if one actor takes the parts of Linda and Dolores and another actor takes the parts of Susan and Mom.

IF YOU FORGET YOUR LINES . . .

★ *If you forget your lines and can't hear the prompter, just think about what your character would say and then* ***ad-lib*** *(say it in your own words).*

THE DIRECTOR

PRAISING THE ACTORS

★ *One of your most important jobs as director is to praise the actors. Watch for good things that happen during rehearsals and make them part of the finished performance. The best praise is specific and sincere. Keep a notebook handy for your notes about things to remember and praise.*

One of the director's jobs is to help an actor "get into character" by helping him or her imagine what it would be like to truly be that character. How would a character show joy or anger? For example, would one character show joy by laughing aloud while another smiled quietly? Would a character stamp her foot in anger or turn her back?

Encourage the actors to practice walking and talking as their characters. How would the main character of the play walk? How would her voice change when she is happy or upset? Helping the actors find answers to these kinds of questions will create a more believable performance.

BLOCKING THE ACTION

As the director, you help the actors plan how to move when they are onstage. This is called *blocking the action*, and it usually takes place during rehearsal. The script sometimes tells the actors how and when to move, but it is your job to give additional directions. You also give the actors little signs, or *cues*, about when to go onstage and offstage.

When you are blocking the action, try to use the whole stage. Important action should take place near the front of the stage, close to the audience.

Actors should face the audience most of the time when they're speaking, so the audience can see the actors' faces and hear their lines. But sometimes you might ask an actor to turn away to show sadness or rejection.

KEEPING THE PLAY MOVING

Keep the play moving by helping the actors *overlap* their lines. To overlap, an actor says her first word just as the actor before says her last word. Combine overlapping with occasional pauses to make the play more lively and natural.

DIRECTOR'S TIPS

★ *Make sure that all actors speak clearly and loudly enough to be heard.*

★ *Help the actors "get into character" by asking questions about what their character is like.*

★ *Remind the actors to relax as they say their lines. Using props will help them move naturally.*

★ *Plan the action so that the audience can see the actors' faces.*

★ *Remind the actors not to stand between other actors and the audience.*

THE CREW

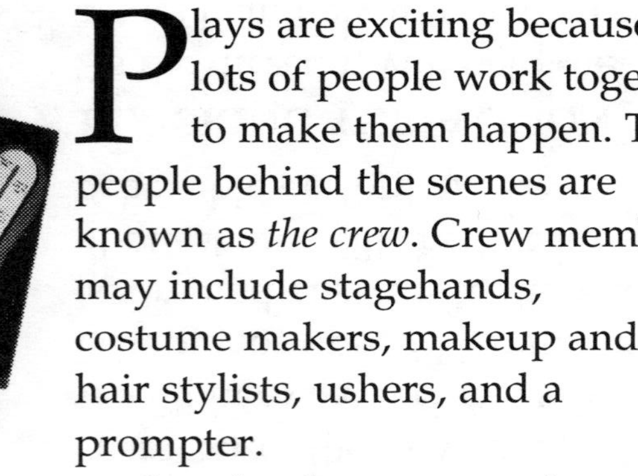

MUSIC AND MOOD

★ *Before the show and during set changes and intermissions, create the mood of the 1940s with Big Band music. Duke Ellington, Louis Armstrong, and Benny Goodman were popular Big Band leaders.*

Just before the play starts, the stagehand in charge of music can ***fade out*** *the music by gradually lowering the volume until it can no longer be heard.*

Plays are exciting because lots of people work together to make them happen. The people behind the scenes are known as *the crew*. Crew members may include stagehands, costume makers, makeup and hair stylists, ushers, and a prompter.

Stagehands create sets by finding, building, and painting scenery. They also change the scenery between acts and operate the curtain.

The *sound crew* creates sound effects and operates the sound system.

The *lights crew* operates the lighting system.

The *stage manager* works closely with the director to manage what happens onstage. He or she marks the script with every sound or light cue and all set changes, and then makes sure every cue comes on time.

The *property master* or *property mistress* is responsible for finding or making properties—or *props*—and for having the props ready at the right time and in the right place. That way, the actors have exactly what they need each time they go onstage.

Costume makers help the actors find or make costumes. *Makeup* and *hair stylists* help the actors put on makeup and style their hair or wigs.

The *prompter* follows the play line by line in a script book and whispers lines from offstage if an actor forgets them.

Ushers take tickets and lead the audience to their seats. They are sometimes in charge of getting playbills, programs, and tickets ready for the show.

At the end of the performance, everyone who helped put on the show should take a bow at the curtain call!

THE COSTUMES

COSTUME TIPS

★ *The very simplest way to identify characters doesn't even require costumes! An actor can wear a sign around his or her neck with the character's name printed large enough for the audience to read. This way, actors can easily switch parts without having to switch costumes!*

Costumes help bring a play to life and identify characters—but you can have a great performance without costumes, too!

Molly's school clothes.

Molly always wears glasses and usually has her hair in braids. In Act One, she wears school clothes—a simple skirt and sweater, knee socks, and shoes. In Act Two, she wears a sweater and a hula skirt. In Act Three, Molly wears play clothes—jeans and a flannel shirt. Her friends Linda and Susan wear costumes similar to Molly's in each act.

Linda's hula outfit.

Linda wears the same kind of clothing that Molly does in each act.

Susan's play clothes.

Susan dresses like Molly and Linda in each act, but she wears a bulkier sweater with her Halloween costume.

Ricky's play clothes.

Ricky wears blue jeans, a long-sleeved shirt, a sweater vest, and high-top basketball shoes in Act One and Act Three. In Act Two, he is dressed as a pirate.

Dolores wears a knee-length skirt, a cardigan sweater over another sweater of a matching color, bobby socks, and loafers.

Mom wears a housedress and high heels. In Act Two, she wears a sweater over her dress.

Dolores's costume. *Mom's costume.*

QUICK CHANGES

★ *Practice making quick costume changes. An actor playing both Linda and Dolores can put the hula outfit over her school clothes in Act Two. Then, in Act Three, she can quickly remove the hula outfit, change to Dolores's loafers, and put on Dolores's cardigan sweater.*

★ *An actor playing both Susan and Mom can change costumes quickly by pulling Mom's dress and sweater over Susan's costume and exchanging Susan's shoes for Mom's high heels.*

Stage Sets

Scenes

★

ACT ONE
The McIntires' backyard on a sunny fall afternoon

•

ACT TWO
The McIntires' backyard on Halloween evening

•

ACT THREE
The McIntires' backyard, the next morning

War on the Home Front has only one set—the McIntires' backyard. One way to create the background for your set is by using large paper to make a mural. Light-brown paper across the back of your stage works best. You can make cutouts to pin or tape to your background. Or make cardboard cutouts that can stand out against the background mural. Use paint or chalk to add details on the cutouts and mural. Applying paint with a large sponge is fast and adds texture.

You can make cutout bushes by using large pieces of cardboard that you paint and tape to or lean against a box, stool, or chair. Or you could make easel backs to support them, as shown. Another way to make bushes is with brown paper bags. Crumple the bags and fill them partway with crumpled newspapers. Paint

them lightly with green paint. Put several together to create bigger or higher bushes.

If you do not have an actual basketball hoop for your set, Ricky can dribble the ball on the stage and pass it to a stagehand behind the scenes when he pretends to shoot a basket. The stagehand can bounce or toss the ball back to Ricky from offstage.

Lighting

You can use lights to set the mood. It is a bright and sunny afternoon during Act One. Act Two takes place in the evening, as it is getting dark. Turn on fewer lights, or turn them down lower, but be sure that the audience can still see everything! Act Three takes place in the morning, so it is very bright. If you don't have lights that can go dim, the stagehand in charge of lights can turn lights on or off as needed.

Backyard set.

Make an easel back by taping a cardboard triangle to the back of the bushes.

Props

Props

★

ACT ONE
Schoolbooks
An apple
A basketball

•

ACT TWO
One or two ukuleles
Three trick-or-treat bags
Popcorn balls
Homemade Halloween treats
A few wrapped candies
A hose

•

ACT THREE
Ricky's trick-or-treat bag
A basketball
A bag of clothes

Here are some ideas for making or finding the props for this play.

Decorate brown paper grocery bags for the trick-or-treat bags.

Halloween treats could include apples, popcorn balls, peanuts, suckers, and pieces of wrapped candy. Use real popcorn balls wrapped in waxed paper, or wrap tennis balls in waxed paper.

Ricky is offstage when he sprays water on the girls during Act Two. You can have a hose on the stage, but *don't* use water for this scene! Instead, have the actors act as if they are being soaked by a hose. You could fill a small bag or coffee can with confetti that Ricky could throw while the actors act as if they are being soaked.

Fill a large paper bag with socks, T-shirts, and at least one pair of boys' undershorts. Fill the bag loosely, so the clothes can fly out easily!

The Stage

There are special terms to describe the front, back, and sides of the stage. These terms were used by actors and directors long ago, and are still used today.

Stages used to be built on a slant, with the back part of the stage higher than the front. This angle allowed the audience to see the actors better. The terms *upstage* and *downstage* come from the way the stage slanted. *Upstage* is the area farthest from the audience—the area that used to be higher. *Downstage* is the front of the stage, nearest the audience. An actor standing in the exact middle of the stage is at *center stage.*

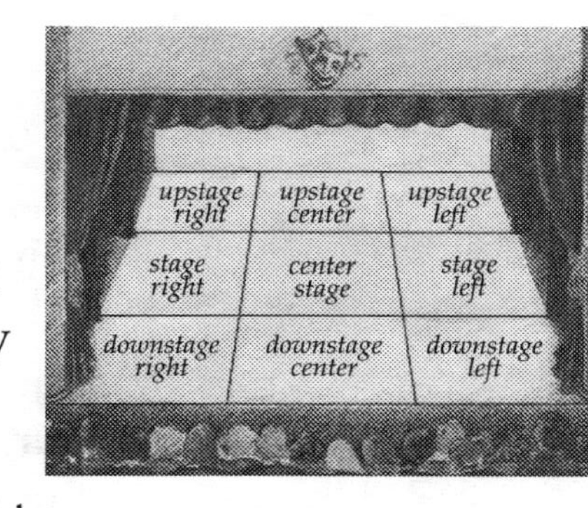

When an actor stands at center stage, facing the audience, the area to the actor's right is *stage right* and the area to the actor's left is *stage left*. The best way to remember *stage right* and *stage left* is to face the audience.

Braids and Hula Skirts

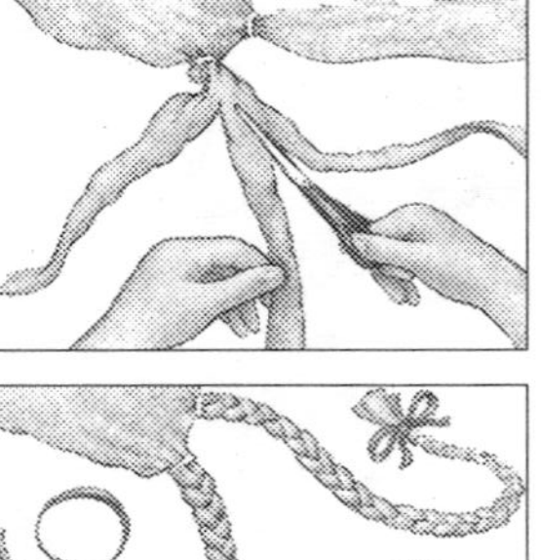

Stocking Braids
Don't braid too tightly! The braids will look better if they are a little loose.

Stocking Braids

Make Molly's braids out of a pair of pantyhose or tights. Fit the waistband around your head, with the legs hanging down your back. Use small rubber bands to mark where each braid will start. Then take the stockings off your head and—starting at the toe—cut each leg into three long strips, up to the rubber band. Braid each leg and tie the ends with ribbons.

Hula Skirt

You can make a hula skirt out of newspaper and crepe paper as Molly did, or you can make one out of tissue paper. Find tissue paper from a large clothing or gift box or buy a package of green tissue paper.

Lay out 3 or 4 layers of tissue paper for the front of the skirt and the same number of layers for the back. Staple the layers together along the top. Use scissors to cut 1-inch strips from

the bottom to about 4 inches from the top, as shown. Tape the front and back together along the 4 inches at the top. Then use a paper punch to punch a row of holes 3/4 inch from the top of the tissue paper. Make the holes about 1 inch apart. Thread a 36-inch length of ribbon or string in and out of the holes, tie your swishy skirt around your waist, and start to dance!

If you have white tissue paper, you could color it green with markers, crayons, or paint. Or, after you have cut the tissue paper, you could staple green crepe paper along the top of your skirt before you punch the holes.

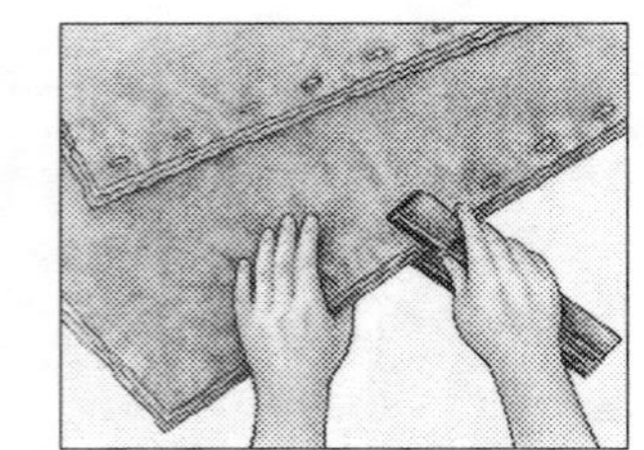

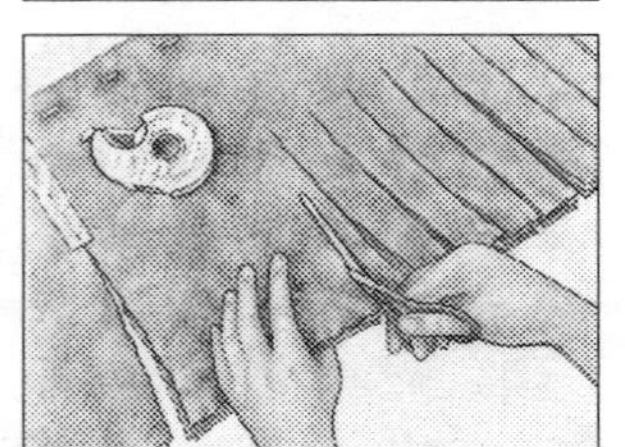

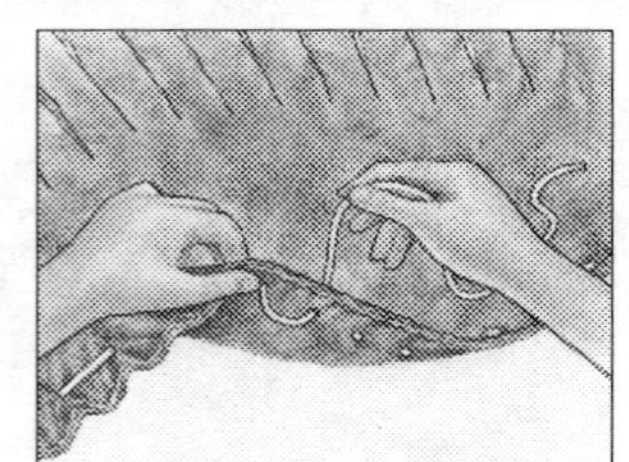

Hula Skirt
The more sheets of tissue paper you use, the fuller your hula skirt will be.

APPENDIX A

Guest Profiles for the Radio Talk Show
Blackline Master

Molly has had a hard time with her mother gone all day during the war. The housekeeper is okay, but now that the war is over Molly wants Mom to be at home and things to return to "normal"—like they were before the war.

Ricky would like Mom to be at home, but he sort of understands why she wants to continue working. After all, she's really enjoyed it, and from his point of view, the McIntire kids have done all right while she's worked.

Mrs. McIntire, mother of Molly and Ricky, loves her job at the Red Cross. She has learned new skills, gained self-confidence, and she feels that she is contributing to society. She also likes being able to contribute to the family's income. She loves her children, but feels they are well looked after by the housekeeper and that it has done them good to be more self-reliant. She wants to be able to enjoy being both a mother and a worker.

Hank is a returning soldier who wants Mrs. McIntire's job. He needs the job to support his family, and feels that because Dr. McIntire already earns a good income, it's unfair—and unpatriotic—for Mrs. McIntire to take a job, too. He feels that after all he has sacrificed at war, he deserves to have the job he wants. He also thinks that mothers should stay home and take care of their children.

Mrs. McIntire's boss at the Red Cross wants Mrs. McIntire to stay on as an employee. She is one of the best employees he's ever had, and he doesn't understand why she and other women can't continue working and raising children, as they did so well during the war.

The psychologist believes that a woman's place is in the home and with her children, and that Mrs. McIntire is being selfish and unnatural in her desire to keep her job.

APPENDIX B

Character Descriptions for the Adult Illiteracy Activity
Blackline Master

Momma is Mrs. Ruth Walker, who is about 32 years old. She is a former slave from North Carolina. She is a very skilled seamstress, but she is illiterate. She was just fired from her job at Mrs. Ford's dress shop because she delivered a package to the wrong address—for the second time. She is now interviewing for another job as a seamstress.

Mrs. Standards is a respectable and wealthy woman from Philadelphia's upper-class Society Hill. She is looking for a skilled seamstress to come to her home to make a number of fancy dresses for the upcoming holiday season for herself and her many daughters. The seamstress will have to travel to Pittsburgh for some of the fittings, and Mrs. Standards must have someone who can travel by herself—which means being able to read railroad schedules.

Put the Story Back into History!

AMERICA AT SCHOOL®

A Unit That Integrates Social Studies, Literature, and Language Arts

In the innovative unit ***America at School,*** girls and boys get to explore the school experiences of five lively fictional girls from America's past, comparing them to their experiences today. Use this creative set of teaching materials to help you integrate your curriculum in a fun and easy way.

The unit features a **Teacher's Guide** with 36 blackline masters, **5 American Girls School Stories, 20 Activity Cards, 2 Giant Wall Charts,** and **10 Poster Maps**. Students discover how our country has changed during the past 225 years by focusing on a world they know well—school. Vivid characters and exciting adventures appeal to both girls and boys—and put the story back into history.

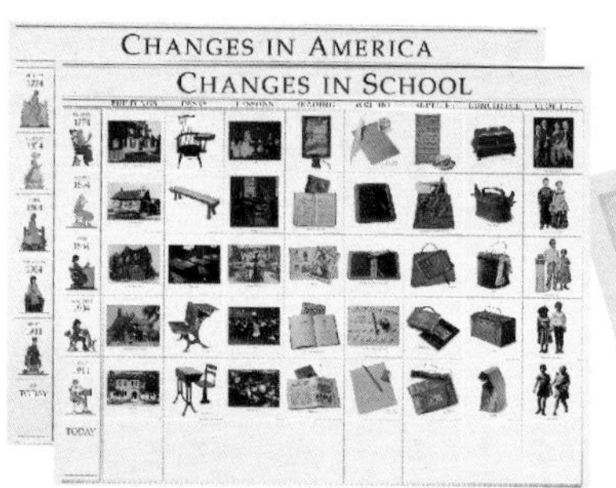

2 GIANT WALL CHARTS

5 SCHOOL STORIES

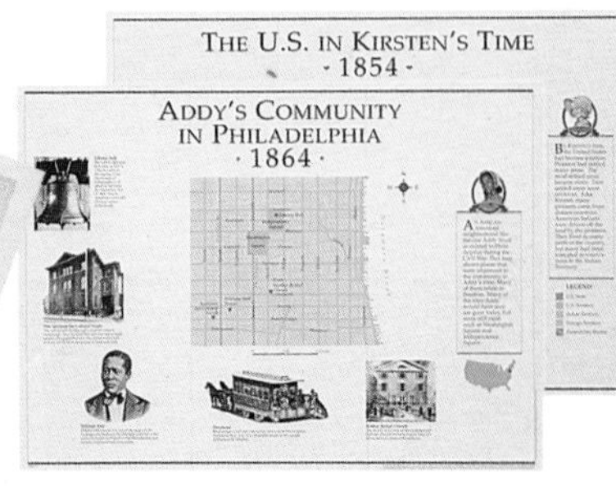

10 POSTER MAPS

20 ACTIVITY CARDS

NO POSTAGE NECESSARY IF MAILED IN THE UNITED STATES

BUSINESS REPLY MAIL

First-Class Mail Permit No. 1137 Middleton, WI USA

POSTAGE WILL BE PAID BY ADDRESSEE

PO BOX 620991
MIDDLETON WI 53562-0991

Get a FREE School/Library Catalogue Today!

Learn more about teacher resources for The American Girls Collection. Return the reply card, or call **1-800-350-6555**.